Adult Children of Alcoholics

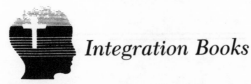 *Integration Books*

STUDIES IN PASTORAL PSYCHOLOGY,
THEOLOGY, AND SPIRITUALITY
Robert J. Wicks, General Editor

also in this series

Clinical Handbook of Pastoral Counseling edited by R. Wicks,
R. Parsons, and D. Capps
Adolescents in Turmoil, Parents Under Stress by Richard D. Parsons
Pastoral Marital Therapy by Stephen Treat and Larry Hof
The Art of Clinical Supervision edited by B. Estadt, J. Compton and
M. Blanchette
The Art of Passingover by Francis Dorff, O. Praem
Losses in Later Life by R. Scott Sullender
Pastoral Care Emergencies by David K. Switzer
Christointegration by Bernard J. Tyrrell
Spirituality and Personal Maturity by Joann Wolski Conn
Choosing Your Career, Finding Your Vocation by Roy Lewis

Adult Children of Alcoholics:

Ministers and the Ministries

Rachel Callahan, C.S.C.
Rea McDonnell, S.S.N.D.

Integration Books

paulist press/new york/mahwah

BV
4463.6
C34
1990

Library of Congress Cataloging-in-Publication Data

74658320

Callahan, Rachel.
    Adult children of alcoholics: ministers and the ministries/by Rachel Callahan, Rea McDonnell.
        p.   cm.—(Integration books)
    Includes bibliographical references.
    ISBN 0-8091-3120-X
    1. Adult children of alcoholics—Pastoral counseling of.
I. McDonnell, Rea. II. Title. III. Series.
    BV4463.6.C34   1990
    253.5'2—dc20
                                                    89-39958
                                                    CIP

Published by Paulist Press
997 Macarthur Boulevard
Mahwah, New Jersey 07430

Printed and bound in the
United States of America

Contents

To our mothers:
Lil and Marie,
Rose and Mildred,
Ruth and the aunts

Foreword

A number of years ago the term "burnout" was very popular because it labeled and opened for discussion an area that had not been given adequate attention. Such can be said of the interest today in ACoA (Adult Children of Alcoholics). The term refers to a now popular issue that had for years been treated indirectly and inadequately.

However, I do have a problem with the term. Although ACoA accurately refers to those persons who were raised in a household in which at least one of the parents or significant persons were alcoholics, the ACoA material contains a wealth of information that is not solely restricted to alcohol-related problems. In a similar vein, to say that this book by Rachel Callahan and Rea McDonnell deals only with pastoral ministry to adult children of alcoholics is to sell it short.

To be sure, it does in fact deal carefully and completely with the psychological and spiritual issues involved in achieving an understanding of, and becoming involved in, ministry to ACoAs. There is however a greater gift that the ACoA literature in general and the work of Callahan and McDonnell in particular have given us. It has helped us to appreciate a broader spectrum of issues such as the implications involved in, and the many factors that are relevant to, the treatment of the subtle problems which result from growing up in a dysfunctional family.

Basic family systems theory and the spirituality which flows with it have often remained hidden from those wishing to be involved in effective self-ministry and/or in providing a sound helping relationship for others in need. The secrets and denial that mark dysfunctional families were left unexamined and the distorted feelings and cognitions which needed expression and correction remained hidden.

To many of us who have been in dysfunctional families and/or have had to deal with others close to us who have thus suffered, the ACoA literature became a true invitation to open up new doors to self-understanding and the appreciation of the often confusing plight

1

of others. And in this beautiful work by Rachel Callahan and Rea McDonnell which combines the work of a psychologist and spiritual director-pastoral psychotherapist, this invitation is especially sound and encouraging.

This book offers us a great deal of information. And it offers us a very important element for any form of healing; it offers us *hope*. The psychological information available about being raised in a dysfunctional family is there for our use and it helps us focus on ourselves as we try to understand what the ACoA literature can tell us about others. It is a true gift, then, for those of us who wish in simplicity to follow God and to take seriously the exhortation "to rouse each other to love and good deeds" (Heb 10:24). And so, I feel it deserves a place not just in the personal libraries of pastoral care personnel, but also in the libraries of any adult Christian who wishes to employ practical information that effectively integrates current psychological findings with contemporary spirituality.

Robert J. Wicks
Series Editor

Introduction

One of the most recent major shifts in the tentative dance between psychology and religion is the new appreciation which therapists are expressing for the ministers' easy access to those emotionally, mentally, and spiritually pained people who only occasionally seek professional help. In this century, ministers of various denominations have sat at the feet of behavioral scientists, especially through the valued clinical pastoral education (CPE) required in most seminaries. If, at times in the past, training programs in pastoral counseling were no more than courses in psychology offered by the ordained, now pastoral counseling is vigorously naming and claiming its origins in the relationship between human suffering and divine compassion, its origin as ministry.

Ministry is simply service. The minister is one gifted by the Spirit to serve and to build up the community of the faithful. Modeled on Jesus' own ministry of preaching good news and healing the brokenhearted, ministry flows from the Spirit's call and gifts poured out in baptism. Each baptized Christian, then, is gifted for some form of service, some way to continue Jesus' teaching and healing ministry.

> The Spirit of the Lord has anointed me to bring good news to the poor, to set captives free, to restore sight to the blind, to let the broken victims go free . . . (Lk 4:18).

Most of us minister in simple, ordinary ways of friendship, family, work, using the Spirit's gifts to us to support and strengthen the various relationships which we call community, church, the body of believers, the body of Christ. Some of us are "set aside" by the community for the service of leadership in this pastoral care. Some may be ordained to that leadership. In other cases, the community may recognize the specially gifted and come, one by one or in groups, for teaching or healing. This book is addressed to all those

3

baptized who continue Jesus' healing ministry, but especially to those engaged in full-time service of the Christian community.

The newly emerging ministry to adult children of alcoholics (ACoA) is our focus, although much of this is also applicable to those adults who grew up in a dysfunctional family. In our first section we will explore some key concepts, for example, some major paradigm shifts in the field of alcohol and addiction studies. We will offer overviews of the newly-named phenomenon of co-dependency, of the ACoA movement, and of family systems theory. We will focus the issue and provide a working definition of some pivotal ideas.

Next, we will ask each reader to reflect on his or her family awareness and psychological self-awareness, using questions for reflection and journaling. Spiritual self-awareness is a must for a minister hoping to help those who know that their healing lies with their "higher power," however they may image or name their God. Spiritual self-assessment is not the point of the reflection exercises, just awareness which, when accepted, flows into deeper spiritual authenticity.

After a focus on the minister, in Part III we will treat the ministry to those adult children from dysfunctional families. Because ministers are often called on in crises we will review principles of crisis intervention before dealing with the long-term process of healing. A minister, ordained or non-ordained, may be invited to journey toward recovery with an abused adult child. Preaching, teaching, leading youth groups or worship, caring for elderly or outcast populations, may trigger an invitation to the minister to walk with an adult child. Two specific areas of ministry, pastoral counseling and spiritual direction, may be most useful in long-term healing.

Ministers do not always need to wait to be invited. They can take the initiative in inviting adults, especially through preaching and adult educational programs, to inner healing. Healing of the neglected and abused "child within," for example, can release stores of energy for the good, can strengthen family bonds, wash away past resentments, lead to truth and freedom in love, work and church relationships. As Rev. Michael Rokas claimed in his address to the diocesan convention as reported in the November 1986 *Maryland Church News* of the Episcopal Diocese of Maryland:

> The one problem that probably affects more people in the room than any other, the largest common denominator that we share, is the problem related to the disease of alcoholism and chemical addictions. I do not think that my parish is

unique in that most of the pastoral situations that I am involved with on a day to day basis are in some way related to alcohol or other drug problems. The problems often disguise themselves in other ways, but the basis is still the problem with alcohol or another mind-altering drug.

This book will attempt to bridge both what has been experienced and articulated in the popular movements (AA, Alanon, ACoA) and what continues to happen in the different fields of research on alcoholism and its impact on the family. They do not always coincide. This is a book written both for those ministers who have grown up in a family in which alcohol was a problem and for those ministers who work with such adults. In many instances, we are one and the same.

PART I
Focusing the Issue

Chapter 1

Key Concepts

In the last few decades, major paradigm shifts have occurred in the field of alcoholism and addiction studies. This is a field in which there has been a fair amount of painstaking research over the past several decades. This data has produced a veritable explosion of popular literature in the past ten years. The popular literature is now giving voice to the survivors, adult children of alcoholics, for whom a cardinal rule was silence and secrecy. Although the movement had been seeded in Al-Anon and Ala-teen support groups and had gained much momentum during the late 1970s, it was not until February 1983 that the National Association for Adult Children of Alcoholics was formed.

One of the blessings of the Adult Children of Alcoholics movement is that it has popularized a vocabulary and offered a community for many adults other than ACoA. A number of ill-at-ease adults have grown up in dysfunctional families in which alcohol per se was not a problem. Yet these "adult children" report that inconsistency, secrecy, problems with boundaries, inadequate parenting, etc. sowed the seeds for adult problems in behavior and relationship to self, others, and God.

Alcoholism and the Alcoholic

The field of alcoholism and society's perception of it has changed somewhat over the past four decades. E.M. Jellinek is considered the "father of scientific alcoholism research."[1] His ground-breaking lectures at Yale during the late 1940s on the course of alcoholism as an illness are familiar to many of us in ministry. Even as the disease concept of alcoholism[2] was being formulated, however, alcoholism continued to be viewed primarily as a moral problem, a failure of will. Many of us are old enough to remember well the stigmas which were attached to alcohol abuse. "Plastered," "pie-eyed," "boozed up" are some of the words which the neighbors might whisper even as they smirked and/or shunned anyone whose drinking problem was visible outside the home. Those who lived in a family in which alcohol was regularly or periodically abused (and there are 28–34 million of these in the United States) know the confusion and shameful anguish from the inside. We ministers have heard or can tell our own stories about how the situational pain of alcoholism was overlaid by the church's or society's moral judgment. For example, abuse of alcohol stoked many a "fire and brimstone" sermon.

Preachers, teachers and other authorities reinforced the shame which such moral judgments provoked. For example, one man who ministers now, apparently a very bright, successful educator, has a self-esteem quotient in the negative numbers cubed. He tells his story of growing up with a mother who abused alcohol and consequently kept the children looking like ragamuffins. The child's teachers, in a religious school, used to whisper about "the drunk." These "ministers" sadly drove deeper the child's self-loathing and his experience of learning to distrust radically his own experience of reality.

This ACoA tells of being in second or third grade when something was stolen from a classmate. He had not taken it, but he was picked out of line and, because of his family's reputation, accused of the thievery. He denied it and yet his teacher continued to blame him. When no one owned up to the stealing, the teacher announced that the thief's hands would turn black for lying as well as stealing (a commentary on the subtlety of racial prejudice in the 1940s). The ACoA remembers vividly his anxiety during the afternoon when, despite his certitude that he had not taken the item, he waited, trembling, staring at his hands, expecting them to turn black. Alcoholism was attacked in this situation as moral failure and "the sins of the mother" were visited on the child.

It was not until 1955 that the American Medical Association formally recognized that alcoholism is a disease. Yet as recently as 1987 a study reports that despite the increasing public awareness of alcoholism as a disease, there remains still a strong ambivalence in which alcoholism continues to be viewed as moral failure. The 1988 Supreme Court decision, allowing the Veterans' Administration to refuse medical benefits for alcoholism treatment, compounds the ambiguity.

Not only in mainstream culture, but in various subcultures, there are also varying perceptions of alcoholism as a problem. For example, an abnormally high percentage of native American high school (50%)

and college (80%) students drop out of school because of alcoholism. They receive conflicting messages that drinking is an acceptable male behavior and yet, when problematic, a disorder of the spirit, rather than a disease, and therefore subject to judgment and worthy of punishment. In the Hispanic sub-culture a tradition of respect for elders shores up the natural defense of denial, the denial that the adult's drinking is a problem. Consequently the disease, which is progressive, often does not get identified until its later stages.

Popular literature suggests an uncomplicated genetic source of alcoholism. Certainly statistics bear out that adult children of alcoholics seem more vulnerable to addictive behaviors than a comparable non-ACoA population. Biological findings about the offspring of alcoholics, however, have been inconsistent. Alcoholism is a complex phenomenon which also includes environmental, social and personal variables other than genetic makeup.

Alcoholism is certainly a physical disease which is both chronic and progressive. Physical symptoms, however, are the last to appear. If left untreated, alcoholism will end in insanity or premature death. Helping an alcoholic be convinced that he or she suffers from a disease rather than moral failure may at least break the cycle of shame which leads to further drinking.

Shame is a prevailing emotion for the alcoholic. As once society hid the disease of cancer, as once the person who was suffering from this disease often refused to admit it or treat it or talk about it, so now the alcoholic defends and denies, usually on a grand scale. Moralizing, even simple religious talk, often compounds the shame, and is not effective as an intervention. While a minister may be part of an intervention, which is that community effort to get an alcoholic to agree to treatment, sometimes the official representative of the church at that crucial moment is counter-productive, simply because of the overlay of morality associated with organized religion.

Yet alcoholism is a spiritual disease as well as a physical illness. It destroys one's relationship with God just as it destroys love and work relationships. Alcoholics may be fired from their jobs, families may go through divorce. However, there is no divorce of the alcoholic, no firing by God. Indeed, God as higher power is the only medicine which heals this disease.

The story of the prodigal son (Lk 15:11–31) offers a paradigm for healing. It is only when the son "comes to his senses" that he can start home where the father (the symbol of God) is watching for his return. Because spirituality is the first area of one's life to be attacked by this disease, it is usually the last to be healed. First the alcoholic must come enough to his or her senses to start treatment with the Twelve Steps of Alcoholics Anonymous. These Twelve Steps are a spiritual program, a vehicle of societal grace in our culture. Once the alcoholic has regained "senses," God, who will not interfere with human freedom, can rush down the road to welcome the one thought "dead, but who is alive again."

Those who work with the diseased respect the power of the disease. After two or three years of "working the program" (the Twelve Steps), emotional health returns. For serenity, peace of mind and heart, the alcoholic needs about five years of consistently turning one's will and entire life over to God (the third step). There are no quick solutions, no bandaids to cover these wounds.

The alcoholic is a good person who is infected by an insidious disease, repeats author Patti McConnell (pseud.).[3] "No one will be blamed," she assures her ACoA readers. While there are many medical tests for a variety of diseases, alcoholism cannot yet be measured by blood tests or liver scans. While there are many self-diagnosing tests for alcoholism printed periodically in popular magazines, further observation indicates that even the "infallible sign" of alcoholism, disruption of relationships and inability to work, no longer points out the "functional alcoholic." Some alcoholics *do* work every day and maintain some semblance of relationship, superficial and/or withdrawn as it may be.

Mood change may now be a more accurate indicator of disease. For example, one ACoA noted that her mother's first sip of alcohol each evening brought out a vicious personality which was probably well defended during her daytime activities. A principal of a large school is an outgoing, caring man. His one drink at night leaves him dull and withdrawn. The next morning he functions well again at school.

To summarize: although we lack total genetic proof as of yet of the physicality of alcoholism as a disease, we as a society are beginning to understand it as such. An alcoholic is a good person with an insidious disease. The disease is not only physical but relational and spiritual as well. The best known treatment for it seems to be faithful working of the Twelve Step program and faithful participation in the community of Alcoholics Anonymous.

The Co-Dependent

Co-dependency does not seem to have a physical component, but it is much the same obsessive-compulsive, addictive disease as alcoholism. Co-dependency is that disease in which another or others in a family, community or work situation are addicted to a person, usually the alcoholic or other ill-at-ease person in the "system." Co-dependents, due to a lack of wholeness within themselves, enable the diseased person to depend (co-depend) on them in unhealthy ways and so to progress in their disease. Rather than offering tough love, confrontation or even an authentic, well-grounded self in opposition to the pivotal person's moods and irrational behavior, the co-dependent enablers sacrifice their "selves." They "de-self" for the sake of another.[4] Their "selves" are usually damaged, lacking autonomy, clarity of values, worth or esteem in their own eyes. It is obvious that like alcoholism, co-dependency harmfully affects emotions, relationships and spirituality.

Other current cross-fertilizations, such as the women's movement and the experience of adult children of alcoholics who marry dysfunctional spouses, have provided a widening articulation of co-dependency as a disease entity in itself. Anne Wilson Schaef takes exception to tying the concept of co-dependency too closely to the alcoholic family. She, a major author on the topic, maintains that co-dependency is a broader disease process than can be embraced by the chemical dependency field. She claims that co-dependency is a generic systemic part of the addictive process which shows up in specific problem areas beyond chemical dependency. She stretches our thinking beyond the personal, interpersonal and familial issues spawned by alcoholism and raises the larger and not to be ignored societal question in both of her books: *Co-Dependence: Misunderstood, and Mistreated* (1986) and *When Society Becomes an Addict* (1987). She would argue that to ignore the larger questions regarding co-dependence truncates our understanding of and healing of the more specific manifestations of this disease in the areas of chemical dependence, mental health, family therapy and women's issues.

Many of the characteristics of co-dependency are reinforced by our American and our religious cultures. To be able to name these characteristics gives us a better chance to tame them. Some which Schaef describes include:

a.–**External Referenting.**—This means that instead of trusting one's own experience, feelings, perceptions, a person needs to validate his/her sense of self by checking what others think or feel. Because a person does not have a clear sense of self outside of another person they are vulnerable to staying in a relationship even if it is not a life-giving relationship. Schaef talks about "cling-clung" relationships in which the dependency is so intense that neither believes one can survive without the other.

We live in a society in which "impression management," which Schaef includes as a sub-symptom of co-dependence, has become the national way of life. During the 1980s the United States was governed by a chief executive whose appointment calendar was filled with "photo opportunities." Often the creation and management of perception has become more important than the encouragement of independent thought and the pursuit of truth. On the individual and family level this is articulated as the question, "What will others think?" rather than as encouragement to trust and articulate one's own experience.

b.–**Caretaking.**—Another characteristic of co-dependency outlined by Schaef is caretaking. Traditionally our society has cast women in this role. In an alcoholic family in which mother is the problem drinker, father can often assume that role. Some children in dysfunctional families very early take on this responsibility. Their self-esteem becomes linked with "doing" rather than "being." Self-worth becomes a function of taking care of everybody else right into adult life, and consistently ignoring one's own needs and limits. Very often this leads to a "victim" or "martyr" stance.

c.–**Physical Illness.**—Sometimes the only socially acceptable way in which a co-dependent can get his/her legitimate needs met is through illness. The stress of being a caretaker is enormous, especially if a person never or seldom acknowledges his/her own limits and needs. Workaholics and care-aholics often develop stress-related functional or psychosomatic illness. The pain and discomfort of these illnesses are real but physicians can discover no organic basis for the illness. This further diminishes the self-esteem of the sufferer.

There are other characteristics of co-dependency which are all associated with an inadequate sense of self as separate and worthwhile. Since most of these characteristics are issues for the adult child they will be amplified later in the book.

Treatment of the Family

Just as there has been an evolution, although uneven, in society's perception of the phenomenon of alcoholism, there has also been significant evolution in the treatment of this illness. During the 1960s alcohol treatment began to focus more on family rather than individual treatment. While Alcoholics Anonymous (AA) continues as the most durable vehicle for individual recovery and maintenance of sobriety, family therapy has been a significant, some would argue, the most significant, tool in treatment.

From an interdisciplinary base, deriving originally from treatment of schizophrenics, family therapy has evolved since the 1950s as a major means to deal with less debilitating dysfunctions than schizophrenia. Family therapy became increasingly more focal in the treatment of alcoholics during the 1960s. By the early 1980s the family therapy models of theorists/practitioners like Virginia Satir were cross-fertilized with budding attention to the survivors in alcohol-centered families, ACoA. Popular, but already classics in this new field, are works by Claudia Black, Sharon Wegscheider-Cruse and Janet Woititz which are rooted in understandings from family therapy. For example, it is easy to recognize that Claudia Black's[5] well received ACoA roles of the "responsible one," the "adjuster," the "placator" and the "acting out" one are at least theoretical "kissing cousins" of family therapist Virginia Satir's dysfunctional communication styles:[6] placator, blamer, intellectualizer and distractor. The "hero," the "mascot," the "lost child" and the "scapegoat" are yet other designations.

Family triangles and boundary issues of enmeshment versus separation which continued to be articulated by the Murray Bowen school of family therapy show up with painful flesh and blood reality in ACoA stories of physical or sexual abuse. The vocabulary and concepts which have been articulated by the various schools of family therapy are further explained below.

Basic Concepts of Family Systems Theory

While different schools of family theory use different language and sometimes different emphases, the concepts which they identify in family systems theory are similar. Family systems theory presupposes that no matter what the scenario appears to be, it is the system and not a particular individual that needs intervention and treatment. It is unlike other modalities in which the "identified patient" is the one who is feeling or displaying symptoms and becomes the focus of treatment. The "identified patient" is the person expected to change or be changed. In family systems thinking the entire family is considered the unit of treatment (even though the entire family might not be present for counseling). Often the individual(s) targeted for special coaching are the ones who have the greatest capacity for change.

The concept of identified patient deserves a bit of elaboration. It is the result of often subtle family projections. Some theorists would call this scapegoating. We are familiar with the process of scapegoating in a broad social context where often, for example, a minority group is labeled with society's undesirable qualities. Society creates conditions which make the "self-fulfilling prophecy" occur; for example, society maintains educational discrimination which keeps minorities in an inferior position.

In a family system this projection is often subconscious and subtle. The symptom of the identified patient can take multiple forms and appear anywhere in the family: for example, a child's hyperactivity, school problem, bedwetting; a parent's under- or over-functioning or addiction; a grandparent's premature senility.

In any organic system, even our bodies, *where* the symptom appears is not necessarily the source of the organic difficulty. Jaundice is not an eye problem but a liver malfunction. If a symptomatic person is going to receive treatment, the most efficient way is to involve the entire family. Some family theorists would go so far as to argue that this is the only way to address any dysfunction. Probably most persons in the helping professions who work with individuals would counter with a strong argument that working with an individual to give him or her a greater sense of self in fact empowers an individual to make changes for himself or herself within a system (family, work, church). Such a client would become sufficiently clear about self so as even to be able to leave the system if need be.

This capacity for self-differentiation and determination does not exist for children. Thus if a child is the identified patient it is very important to involve the family as unit of treatment. For example, labeling a child is a process which inhibits rather than enhances freedom for change. A child caught in a label or role, as frequently happens with children in alcoholic families, gets "stuck" in roles that often become like straightjackets in later adult functioning.

Another important concept in family systems thinking is the concept of *balance*. This is called, in technical terms, homeostasis. The recent work which has been done in the articulation and study of co-dependency in an alcoholic family is a fine example of this concept. The important thing to remember is that balance or homeostasis is so important in any system that whatever quirk or symptom which may be observed from the outside is in that system because it serves to enhance the balance of the system. Whenever an individual in the system changes, even in the direction which everyone else apparently desires, probably someone else in the system will behave in a way which is unconsciously designed to restore the former balance to the system. Systems resist imbalance. No matter how uncomfortable, the balance which is familiar is always preferred initially to the discomfort of moving toward a new equilibrium.

Too often the mistake is made that the person who displays a symptom is the weak one. But where a system breaks down depends as much upon position in a system as on anything else.

Self-differentiation is a key concept. Family theorist Murray Bowen would give it the greatest weight.[7] In any family system it is important to assess, hopefully multi-generationally, the amount of self-differentiation which is not only tolerated but fostered. Self-differentiation is a significant issue in an alcoholic family, not only in the area of clear definition of boundaries but especially in the clouding of responsibility and the lack of clarity of definition of self. If an individual can remain a relatively non-anxious "I" and does not need to disappear into the "we" of an anxious system, or fall into the powerless "you" position which places responsibility for change outside, he or she is in the process of self-differentiation. Such a person is being healed of co-dependence.

Many families exert an almost gravitational energy against this process of self-differentiation. Boundaries get fused or merged. This may result in what appears to be a close "we," but often at the expense of one or the other person. Harriet Lerner, a feminist therapist, writes about the process of "de-selfing" which sometimes happens in a marriage: one partner consistently accommodates and gives in to the other, usually with an increasing sense of anger. Anger, however, as Lerner notes, can be very helpful if a person uses it to get a clearer sense of self.[8]

Another concept which family systems offers is the *extended family field*. In today's society, the extended family is less visibly clustered together and the nuclear family appears to be hanging out there on its own. We might mistakenly underestimate the potency of the extended family field unless we allow ourselves to become aware of how strong the umbilical cord of the telephone can be in stirring up feelings! Family patterns and family agendas get passed on from one generation to another, sometimes influenced by sibling position. Perhaps it is the role of caretaker which gets transmitted. Perhaps it is the script that one sibling must overfunction in the care of an aged parent and another underfunction. It might be the pattern of fiercely possessive sisters who resist including their brothers' spouses to the point that the brothers need to cut themselves off from their family of origin to start a new family.

How do some of the concepts defined above actually show up in a family system? To understand this, the concept of emotional *triangles* is a useful one. "When any two parts of a system become uncomfortable with one another, they will 'triangle in' or focus on a third person, or issue, as a way of stabilizing their own relationships with one another."[9]

Triangles are formed to reduce anxiety in one relationship by focusing on a third person. At an unconscious level we pull this third person in to try to lower the emotional intensity in the original relationship. Triangles can occur anywhere, in any system. While ordinarily they involve three persons, an issue can also be involved in a triangle. The important thing to remember is that a triangle functions to keep the original relationship in balance, for example, that of husband and wife. This happens by the way in which the third person relates to each of them or to their relationship.

Let us look at an example of a particularly blatant triangle—a family of three: Dorothy, her husband Sam and their eighteen year old daughter Toni. In this particular family Dorothy is the identified patient. Her husband and daughter project onto her the label of "selfish." From the time Toni was very small, Dorothy and Sam disagreed about child-rearing and discipline. Dorothy never perceived Sam as supporting her attempts to set limits with Toni. She grew resentful of the way in which Sam not only undermined her efforts, but also showered Toni with presents while withdrawing any signs of affection from Dorothy. As Dorothy "let" Sam take over the parenting of Toni, a terrible chasm developed between Dorothy and Toni.

By the time Dorothy sought some help, Toni and Dorothy were not speaking. Toni and her father spent great amounts of time together. Supposedly everyone was upset at this situation in which there appeared to be such dramatic overfunctioning by Sam and underfunctioning by Dorothy in the area of parenting.

It quickly became evident that the close relationship between Sam and Toni kept Sam and Dorothy from dealing with their own issues of intimacy and parenting which were the original cause for anxiety. Can you guess who was the most resistant to working with the family issue? Sam, who had the most to lose: his "good guy" image.

Looking at this further, from a systems point of view, both Dorothy and Sam unconsciously were handing on to Toni some old agendas of their own: Dorothy's very close relationship with her own father and Sam's troubled, distant relationship with his mother.

Another example: Bill is the oldest child in a family in which his father was alcoholic. When Bill's father would be drinking he could become verbally abusive to Bill's mother. He might take her carefully prepared supper and throw it on the floor shouting, "Who could eat this slop?" Bill, wanting to make his mother feel better and assure her how good a cook she was, would often eat extra, sometimes even when he didn't feel like it. In his attempts to defuse the observed tension between his mother and his drinking father, he developed a weight problem which fed into negative self-esteem issues. Although Bill's father stopped drinking before he was a teenager, Bill continued to struggle with self-esteem issues around appearance, even though as he approaches mid-life he is an attractive, well-proportioned man.

Lastly, a word about *secrets*. It is important to be aware of how secrets can function in a family system. The content of the secret is hardly as important as the process. There are many "typical" family secrets: mental illness, illegitimacy, desertion, certain kinds of illness. Of course, very often alcoholism and its effects are "the family secret."

Whatever the content of the secret, it is the process on which we need to focus. Secrets can function as great obstacles to communication. They become vehicles of division and power: who knows, who does not know? Secrets can create false alliances or other problems, such as an unnatural aloofness from the person who is not privy to the secret. Often the family protests that the reason for the secret is to spare someone pain.

The summary above represents some of the key notions contributed by family systems theorists during the last thirty years. They have become very useful in understanding and working with the dysfunction of an alcoholic family.

Emergence of the ACoA Movement

Young children living with an alcoholic parent were the first to receive attention. Social workers, educators, child psychologists noted the impact on children of various factors such as the gender of the alcoholic, the age when the alcoholism appeared, etc. For example, Dr. Robert Ackerman[10] pondered the different types of alcoholism: periodic, binge, and continuous, and its influence on the child. The happy-go-lucky, sentimental alcoholic response to the child was noted over against the angry, abusive alcoholic response.

In 1976 the first written material mentioned the *adult* child who grew up in an alcoholic-centered home and the continuing impact which the disease has in the life of the adult survivor. Claudia Black's *It Will Never Happen To Me* appeared in 1981 as one of the early full-length books to pinpoint the emotional pain in such a family of origin. She also suggested that ACoA have a genetic predisposition to alcoholism themselves, although crying, "It will never happen to me!"

Janet Woititz's *Adult Children of Alcoholics*[11] was published in the same year as the founding of the National Association for Children of Alcoholics (NACoA). In an earlier work, *Marriage on the Rocks* (1979), Woititz highlighted the work of the Center of Alcohol Studies at Rutgers University. She noted, however, that of the 873 references in the Center's bibliography of alcohol education, only 38 dealt with the family's involvement, the effects of the disease on the family.[12]

Book distribution services for ACoA sprang up to cope with their demand for self-understanding. Perrin and Treggett, located in Rutherford, New Jersey, for example, specializes in books on alcoholism and child abuse. Many such bookstores and warehouses providing ACoA and related materials now dot the country.

Throughout this book, we will be amplifying this key concept. We ourselves, as we learn, reflect, minister and reflect again, are ourselves becoming part of the emergence of the ACoA movement.

The Twelve Steps

The Twelve Steps, basic to recovery programs such as AA, Al-Anon, Ala-teen, now expanding to include such groups as Sex and Love Addicts Anonymous, Gamblers Anonymous, Nar-anon (for co-dependents of those abusing narcotics), are not concepts. The Twelve Steps, used frequently in ACoA groups, are experiences— experiences founded on our relationship as creatures with a loving God whose power frees us from addictions and addictive ways of relating and behaving. The Twelve Steps also call for a community of healing, which many compare to a church community, a community centered in Christ, empowered by the Spirit.

We list the Twelve Steps to conclude this introductory chapter.

1. We admitted we were powerless over alcohol—that our lives had become unmanageable.

2. Came to believe that a Power greater than ourselves could restore us to sanity.

3. Made a decision to turn our will and our lives over to the care of God as we understood God.

4. Made a searching and fearless moral inventory of ourselves.

5. Admitted to God, to ourselves and to another human being the exact nature of our wrongs.

6. Were entirely ready to have God remove all these defects of character.

7. Humbly asked God to remove our shortcomings.

8. Made a list of all persons we had harmed and became willing to make amends to them all.

9. Made direct amends to such people wherever possible, except when to do so would injure them or others.

10. Continued to take personal inventory and, when we were wrong, promptly admitted it.

11. Sought through prayer and meditation to improve our conscious contact with God as we understood God, praying only for knowledge of God's will for us and the power to carry that out.

12. Having had a spiritual awakening as the result of these steps, we tried to carry this message to alcoholics and to practice these principles in all our affairs.

PART II
The Minister

Part II will focus on the minister. Hopefully reflection opportunities provided here will enhance our self-awareness on several levels. In order to be helpful to another it is useful to have sensitivity and awareness about our own selves and where our own experiences, needs, feelings, thinking and theology might become obstacles for working with others. If there has been alcohol abuse in our own families of origin we need to be sensitive to how this may impact our work with other ACoA. Unresolved feelings of our own may keep us from being psychologically available to the ACoA or may pre-dispose us to work too hard in efforts to rescue another from pain.

The tone of this section, focused on the minister, is invitational as well as informational. Before gathering any more information and facts from "out there," we invite you to take some time to study your most valuable resource, your own self and your own life-experience. In your pastoral ministry with others you are your most significant human resource. Your own contact will facilitate or hinder whatever information or referral you wish to transmit. Your own ministry of listening or speaking will be enhanced by self-awareness.

Chapter 2

Family Awareness

We were created in relationship . . . and God saw that it was good! Lord, you have probed me and you know me. You understand my thinking and feeling. . . . You knit me in my mother's womb. I give you thanks that I am wondrously made. When my bones were being formed, carefully formed in my mother's womb, when I was growing there in secret, you knew that I was there . . . (Ps 139).

In order to enhance self-awareness for more positive ministry you will be invited to explore some of your own family history in order to be able to answer the question: Who are you? Who is the real self that you bring into all of your relationships and work?

We do not make this journey alone. As you start these exercises ask the Spirit to bring into your awareness the truth which you are able to hear, trusting this truth gradually to set you free.

As ministers we are a people whose Judaeo-Christian heritage is an invitation to remember, especially to remember God's setting our "family" free. After many sufferings and much survival our people have found God to be faithful "all the way to this place."

Moses said to the people: "The Lord will lead you. . . . You remember how God brought you safely all the way to this place just as a parent would carry a child" (Dt 1:30–31).

As you embark upon this first step of your family awareness, pause for a moment and rest in the words of this passage. Whatever our family history, no matter what its mixture of pain and joy, the Lord has brought each one of us to the place where we are in our own history. We know from our own stories and from the stories we hear that our God is not a God who rescues us from pain and suffering, but a God who is with us and shares our vulnerability.

One of the paradoxes of the Twelve Steps is that precisely

through a spirituality of powerlessness and surrender we discover within us the strength of God. God is with us even in what appears to be divine powerlessness in the face of human suffering. The God-who-is-with (Emmanuel) can only become present and active in human suffering when we are with—in our listening, receiving and loving another in his or her story.

In this family awareness section we will offer you a tool to tell your own story to yourself. This tool can complement the more famil-iar tools of writing an autobiography or using journaling techniques.

As an initial step in self-awareness you are invited to "put your-self into context." Hopefully, you can adapt these exercises in your own ministry with adult children. The exercises presented in this chapter are culled from the work of family theorists and therapists spanning the last twenty-five years.

Prior to understanding some of the rules and roles we learned as children it is helpful to gather some data about our own family struc-ture and to identify persons who have had a significant impact upon us. There are different ways of doing this. We will describe the genogram. As you work with this, it is also helpful to jot down the influences of the larger culture—global, national, regional, ethnic, religious, etc. Get curious about how these may or may not have impacted your own family of origin.

Genogram

This exercise involves developing and understanding your own family root system. Family trees have long been used in history, and the past fifteen years have seen renewed popular interest in genea-logical history, which is so much more than tracking names and dates. Family therapists have learned the utility of working with genograms as a way to organize and understand large amounts of data about family structures and interactions. A recent comprehensive work in the area is provided by Monica McGoldrick and Randy Gerson in their book *Genograms in Family Assessments.*[1] Although there is no firm agreement yet, alcoholism in family genes seems to have an impact on subsequent generations. Alcoholism in grandparents can influence the adult child, perhaps genetically, but definitely because the adult child's parent is an ACoA.

Since the genogram is intended to give a comprehensive, quick visual history of a family system we will illustrate the symbols used to describe the basic family membership and structure.

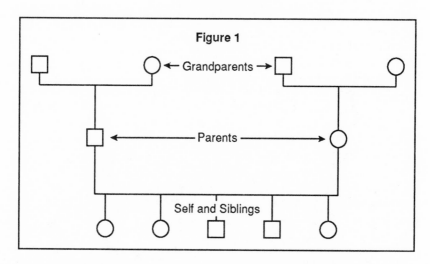

Figure 1

The basic symbols used in a genogram are fairly simple:

□ = Male

○ = Female

⊠⊗ = Died. Insert the year, age and cause of death next to symbol

m = Married. Write in the year and place

\# = Divorced. Write in date

⚯ = Separated. Write in date

= = Close bond between two members of family

⋀⋁ = Conflict between family members

A, D, E = Alcohol, drug or eating disorder. Write this letter on top of the symbol for the person with that disorder

PA, SA = Physical or sexual abuse. Put these letters on top of the symbol for that person

Work the genogram on a large sheet of paper so that you can write major life events or brief descriptions next to the person's name. Here is a sample. (See figure 2). For our purposes, note the **A** for alcoholism recurring on both sides of the family.

As you construct your own genogram you will be looking for family structure, that is, the actual composition of your childhood household, including data about the age and order of you and your brothers and sisters. If there are unusual family configurations these should be noted, for example, another person living in the household or persons outside the house who were primary caretakers of the

Figure 2

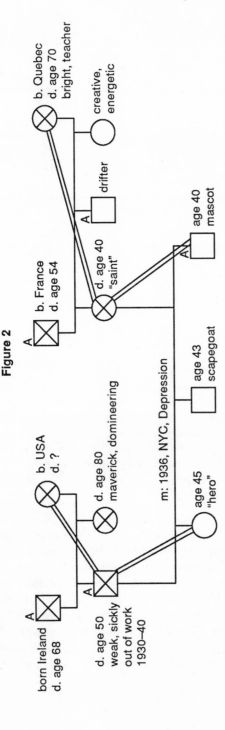

Myths: "If you don't talk about it, it isn't real."
        "It's not OK to make mistakes."
        Alcohol doesn't exist; it's hidden.

Roles: Women are expected to be the strong ones.

Scripts: Nice girls never get angry (don't feel).
        Don't talk to any strangers (don't trust).
        If you can't say something good about someone, don't say anything (don't talk).

children. Pregnancies, miscarriages or abortions, and adoptions should be noted. Death, divorce, remarriage, and change of custody need also to be noted. Genograms of a contemporary family can become quite complex!

Working with a genogram involves more than simply gathering data about the structure of a family system. The other rich data which this picture can give us is information about significant life events, and also data about patterns of functioning and relationship which may repeat themselves across generations.

Placing the family system within the context of the cultural and ethnic background can yield data about family folkways, values, and beliefs. The religious background is often a significant formative factor, perhaps more especially in a minister's family of origin.

Just as it is useful to try to identify the impact of the historically decisive events of the larger culture on the family, it is important to identify the historically decisive events within one's own family, for example, deaths or crisis events such as physical moves or job changes. Vocational histories of family members can be helpful.

What are the family myths? What are the roles of men and women? Are there any sex-specific scripts in the family, for example, "Little boys do not cry"? Are there any family secrets such as alcohol or drug abuse, physical or sexual abuse, unwanted pregnancies?

Another interesting thing to notice is whether or not names are significant. Who named you? For whom have you been named? Have you ever heard "You are just like . . ." How do you hear this—as a compliment? a challenge? a put-down?

Another piece of information which can be visualized in a genogram are patterns of closeness or distance. What are some of the rules governing closeness or distance in your family? Are there significant triangles in the family?

Now, using the data which can be extracted from working with a family root system, you are ready to do some work on your own. Draw a genogram for your own family of origin, one for your mother's and one for your father's families. If you are not sure of dates of births, deaths, marriages, etc. put a question mark next to your guess about the date. For each person jot down a couple of adjectives and a descriptive phrase or adjective to describe the patterns of relationships. For the genograms of your parents' families you may have to do a little data gathering with older members of your family. Be aware that each person has his or her own perceptions which may be subtly or quite dramatically different. When two sisters were asked to describe their aunt, for example, one responded "thrifty and economical" and the other responded "stingy and tight"—nuanced but similar perceptions! Interview your family members if possible to gather as much data as you can.

When you have finished collecting your family data, take some time to let it speak to you. Spend as much time as you need.

Chapter 3

Psychological Self-Awareness

Having reflected upon your family of origin, you are now invited to some reflective exercises to broaden your own understanding of self, particularly your self as minister.

As in the earlier section, take some time to relax as you move into this exercise, center yourself, let yourself become aware of your breathing. Trust that the Spirit is breathing in you and leading you into whatever new or old truths you are about to discover. Ask the Lord to help you believe the good news that God loves you just the way you are, even in those ways you find most painful and unacceptable: anxiety, depression or whatever limits your experience because of your human life and history.

■ In the first part of this exercise make a list of up to ten adjectives which you would use to describe yourself. Ask the Spirit to help you with this list. Do not scrape your consciousness but trust that the truth will "bubble up" from your depths. "Whoever comes to me, rivers of living water will flow from deep within" (Jn 7:37–38). Let the Spirit well up from within and "guide you to all truth."

The aim of the exercise is to try to help you get as clear a sense of your own self as possible. Then, for example, even if everyone in your world considers you a person who can change water into wine and then walk on it, but you feel small and empty inside, you have put down *your* own adjectives. If some outsiders believe you are rash in your actions, but you know yourself to be reflective before acting, you can claim *that* as your truth.

■ Because a part of our self-concept is derived from our interactions with significant others, in this second exercise draw up a list of up to twenty persons who have been and are significant to you. Include your father and mother (or, if either were absent, the person(s) most like father and mother for you), significant siblings, older relatives, teachers, friends, someone you know likes you, someone you know does not like you. Set up your list as follows:

31

	Adjectives	True	False
Mother	_____	_____	_____
	_____	_____	_____
	_____	_____	_____
	_____	_____	_____
	_____	_____	_____

Leave blanks for up to five adjectives which you think the person would use to describe you. When you finish jotting these adjectives for each person's description of you, go back and next to each indicate whether the description is true or false according to *your* own current self-perception.

Compare your two assessments. What do you feel as you look at these lists? Give yourself a little time to let the Lord be with you in this exercise and in whatever you may be feeling. Later on in this chapter you will be invited to look at how your self-concept might impact your ministry.

Feelings

There are a number of different ways to categorize beneficial areas of self-awareness. In the following section we will present some of these categories and again invite you to some quiet or shared reflection.

Feelings and emotions have been written about extensively. Particularly during the 1970s when the human potential movement was cresting in psychology, people were encouraged to "get into their feelings." Sensitivity training groups had as one goal the awareness of and direct expression of feelings. This was a reaction to fairly common patterns of socialization which labeled some feelings "good," others "bad." In general both society and church discouraged expressions of any strong feelings as tasteless or perhaps even sinful, especially any expression of "negative" feelings, such as anger.

Formal educational programs until fairly recently concentrated on cognitive development, to the neglect of teaching persons to experience and integrate the richness of their emotional lives. Consequently, many of us learned to cut off or suppress feelings. At best we may have become aware of them in only the fuzziest kinds of ways.

Feelings are linked with survival at both a physical and a psychological level. Feelings have a physiological component. Probably this can be most dramatically illustrated in a situation in which there is a clear perception of real and present danger. When we perceive a stimulus, whether benign or harmful, as threatening, our perception sets off a whole neuro-endocrine response chain in our bodies which pumps adrenalin into our systems, tightens our muscles and prepares us for the fight or flight response which in earlier days was literally necessary for survival.

Failure to be aware of what is going on inside of us to make appropriate responses often means that our bodies accumulate the stress of unrecognized emotion. Eventually this emotional backlog shows up in a variety of somatic illnesses ranging from headaches to hypertension to various forms of gastro-intestinal disturbances or muscular tension.

If society as a whole has not encouraged us to name and claim our feelings, this is even more true for the adult survivor of troubled homes. There, in our most impressionable years, feelings were to be denied and distrusted and certainly not talked about.

Formal religion has not been very helpful in this area either. Certain feelings have been labeled as bad or sinful. Certainly anger which can be a very useful emotion in helping us to clarify who we are and what we want has been labeled as negative. Even *feelings* of anger have sometimes been classified as sin.

One of the ways in which feelings are useful for us is the way they help us to clarify who we are. While feelings are volatile and change as our perceptions change, they nevertheless deserve our attention.

■ What is the range of your "feeling" vocabulary? How many feeling words can you write down? Again, ask the Spirit to let them bubble up. Take time now to list these feelings.

■ Return to your list and describe how you feel about these feelings. Which feel pleasant? Which unpleasant? Which feelings does your church label positive? negative? How does your church tradition feel about/think about God's emotions? Jesus' emotions? How do you feel about them?

■ Make another list of emotions found in the psalms. Stop and reflect on this list. Would Jesus have prayed cursing psalms in the synagogue? How would God have heard cursing psalms, complaints, arguments, from Israel? from Jesus?

■ Make a list of Jesus' feelings. How would God have looked on Jesus' emotions in all their variety, range of intensity, expression: Jesus' joy, pity, anger, compassion, zeal, longing, love, discouragement, grief, fear?

Fran Ferder, both a clinical psychologist and a doctor of ministry, invites us to a fourfold way of dealing with emotions—noticing, naming, owning, responding.[1] Learning to become more tuned in to some of the bodily correlates of emotion—of heartbeat, muscle tension in various body parts, dryness of mouth, change in body temperature—is the first step. Noticing means attending to subtle and sometimes not so subtle clues that something is going on in our bodies. Focusing and other exercises for enhancing awareness such as those presented in Anthony DeMello's *Saddhana* are helpful.[2]

Once we have noticed what we are feeling, the next step is to be able to name it. Because feelings are subjective and somewhat ephemeral it is sometimes hard to name them. Our "feeling" vocabulary may be constricted. Below are some "feeling" words. How many can you recognize from the inside?

anger

surprise

fear

joy

excitement

surrender

anticipation

How many of these feelings, as you experience them, have range and nuance? A friend used to differentiate her uppermost experience of anger as a "red rage." This was subjectively and expressively quite distinct from mild annoyance!

Are there any feelings which you would be reluctant to claim as your own? Sometimes we place too much "blame" for our feelings outside of ourselves and in doing that we rob ourselves of the capacity to use feelings for change. "You make me so mad and I wish you'd . . ." is qualitatively different from: "I am angry and I need to . . . in order to . . ." In the latter you are "owning" your feelings and allowing them to make clearer whatever response you need to make to a situation.

Responding to feelings does not necessarily mean emoting, dumping or venting feelings. Sometimes the latter only keeps in place whatever circular pattern might be going on in a relationship instead of allowing us to choose a new and freeing response. Keeping in mind that the only person you can change is yourself, then attending to feelings and thinking about what they might be saying or inviting you to is helpful for your survival and growth.

Are there any particular feelings which may get stirred up as ministers working with adult children? Bearing in mind that each of our histories pre-disposes us for certain feelings, let us look at a few. *Compassion*—being with ACoA as they share their painful stories can evoke strong feelings in the listener—sometimes a *sorrow* and *sadness* which bring a lump to the throat, tears to the eyes. Your own emotional history and the degree to which you have worked with it will determine how you experience this. Ask yourself: Are my own boundaries intact enough to keep from being overwhelmed by the sadness and *grief* of another?

Compassion means being with another at a deep level, with (com) their emotions (passion). As the wounds of growing up in an alcohol dominated family begin to heal, the ACoA often experiences and expresses to us some very powerful feelings such as fury, hatred, desire for revenge, despair. Do I *fear* and flinch? How do I respond, be with?

On the other hand, often the experience of growing up in an alcohol dominated family leaves many adult children so guarded and distrustful of their own feelings that we can feel *impatience* with their denial. Or, distrustful also of the safety of relationships, ACoA can be guarded in how they connect with another, withdrawing from the minister, leaving us *confused.* ACoA may cling, hungry for more than compassion; this lack of boundaries can feel quite *disconcerting,* even *threatening* to the minister. How can you, will you, respond?

If as minister you are an ACoA you need to be very aware of the array of feelings which get stirred up inside of you and be careful of overidentification. This is known as countertransference and will be addressed in a separate chapter, "When the Minister Is ACoA."

Cognitive Style

It is incomplete to think about feelings without thinking about perception and cognitive style. There is much evidence which demonstrates that the psychobiological reality of emotions is shaped by how we perceive a stimulus and also by how we think about it. Particularly some of the "negative" emotions such as guilt and depression are influenced by our perception. David Burns, M.D., in his *Feeling Good: The New Mood Therapy,*[3] outlines some of the more typical patterns of automatic negative thinking which predispose a person toward depression. The automatic thinking patterns are often part and parcel of a family agenda which gets passed on through example and socialization. The beauty of learning to identify our own automatic negative thought patterns and learning to correct them with more rational responses is in the simplicity and relative rapidity of change this offers. If you are working with ACoA (or with anyone who is prone to depression) David Burns' book is a valuable self-help tool to add to your library and/or to recommend to persons with whom you work.

Here are some of the common patterns which he describes. See if you can identify with any of them.

1. *All or Nothing Thinking.* This distortion of thinking helps us to simplify the ambiguities of life by viewing reality as a simple matter of black and white, good or bad. It is dangerous in the way that it fosters perfectionism and intolerance of life's basic grayness and ambiguity. In an alcoholic family this pattern of thinking often functions to promote a "saint"/"sinner" scenario. It is difficult, for example, to recognize and name the disease of co-dependency in someone who looks so very perfect. It can be equally difficult to find lovable, good qualities in the alcoholic.

   ■ Reflect on your own patterns of all or nothing thinking. Do you use "absolute" language in your everyday speech, in your public ministry? Are you sensitive to all or nothing thinking when you hear it in the media, used, for example, by politicians and advertisers?

2. *Negative Filter.* This distortion works like a magnet to gather even the slightest negative "filings." An ACoA's college transcript may contain all "A's" except for one "B," but that "B" makes him or her feel like a failure. In a sea filled with good fish, an ACoA might manage to catch the one that is rotten. The glass for some is never half-full, but always half-empty.

   ■ Take some time to see if you yourself use a negative filter and in what circumstances. Do you use it in judging your own performance? Do you use it as a filter for others' reactions to you? Do you use it with God and assume that God uses it with you?

3. *Catastrophizing.* This is a form of negative thinking which assumes the worst. If it were not responsible for so much genuine pain and anguish it might even look amusing. When we catastrophize we know something terrible is going to happen. We assume the worst. If friends are late it is not because they are trapped in traffic but because they are maimed or dead. Catastrophizing predisposes us to live in dread. If things are going undeniably well for an ACoA, the enjoyment of this gets undermined by the internal certitude that something awful is going to happen. Availability to the simple joys of here and now is seriously hampered by this pattern of thinking.

   ■ Reflect on your own pattern of catastrophizing. Do you know anyone who does it well? If either of your parents was a catastrophizer, how did this make you feel and how have you responded to this?

4. *"Mind Reading" Error.* This automatic negative thinking pattern occurs when we assume that we know why another person is acting or reacting a certain way. Someone does not say "good morning" and an ACoA *knows* it is because this person is angry with him or her, or, worse yet, that he or she has done something to offend. It seldom occurs to an ACoA that the person has indigestion or just woke up.

   ■ How and when do you assume what someone else is thinking? Does this pattern operate more or less with colleagues, authorities, parishioners, family?

5. *Personalization.* This cognitive distortion is closely related to mind-reading but probably more damaging to the person who uses it. It is an error learned early in childhood (probably because it was articulated by a parent figure) that we are responsible for how another person feels and acts. If only, for example, an ACoA were a better child (student, wife, mother) the other person, the alcoholic, would feel better and behave differently. An ACoA, because of co-dependency, takes undue responsibility for another's response-ability and so runs himself or herself ragged trying to keep everyone's universe moving smoothly. Because it is common for children to internalize this kind of responsibility and blame themselves for parental limitations, and because the alcoholic family system often pulls children into the co-dependent delusion that if they try harder the parent would not drink, this is a very common automatic negative thinking pattern of ACoAs.

■ For what do you blame yourself? List the situations in "bubble up" fashion, without evaluating them. Stop at ten. Go back and think through: Who is really responsible for _____? Who is responsible for _____'s feeling such and such?

6. *Shoulds.* Getting stuck in a pressure cooker of "shoulds" and "oughts" is another piece of crooked thinking. Unrealistic and unmeetable demands upon the self produce shame and guilt. Unrealistic and unmeetable expectations which we place on others produce anger and resentment against us.

Needs

There are a number of ways to look at needs and to grow in self-awareness of needs. It is important to be able to identify and articulate needs simply because they are so important in human motivation—why we do what we do. Various psychologists have developed "needs" schemas to describe a hierarchy of personal and interpersonal needs. Abraham Maslow describes the hierarchy of needs as survival, safety, security, belonging; then "higher order" needs for truth, beauty and self-actualization.

Henry Murray devised an entire personality theory based upon needs. This has been the foundation of a frequently used psychological test, The Edwards Personal Preference Schedule,[4] which defines and measures the internal hierarchy of needs including:

achievement: doing one's best; being successful
deference: getting suggestions from others; finding out what others think
order: organizing details of work; keeping an orderly environment
exhibition: having others notice one's appearance and what one says
autonomy: being able to come and go; being independent in speech and decisions
affiliation: being loyal and helpful to friends; participating in friendly groups
intraception: being able to figure out one's own and others' motives
succorance: having others to help and encourage us
dominance: to be a leader
abasement: to take blame and feel guilty
nurturance: helping friends and people in trouble
change: doing new and different things

endurance: keeping at a task till finished

heterosexuality: spending time and being in love with someone of the opposite sex

aggression: attacking contrary points of view, criticizing others publicly

Relational Needs

William Schutz[5] developed a simple test, called Fundamental Interpersonal Relations Orientation-Behavior (FIRO-B), based on Timothy Leary's theory about the basic interpersonal needs of inclusion, control, and affection.

Inclusion. Inclusion reflects the need to belong, to be accepted into groups or actively to invite others to join one's own group. It is not unusual for a person to measure higher on the scale of wanting inclusion than on the scale of expressing inclusion behaviors to others.

Control. In almost any dyadic or group relationship, control becomes an issue. We differ in our need for control or our desire to be controlled and/or led. Between the extreme poles of "autocrat" and "abdicrat" there are nuances and differences. Sometimes the need varies according to the group or situation. Control is often an issue for anyone who grew up in a family where he or she felt that things were out of control or that he or she was a victim.

Affection. Affection simply means the basic need to give and receive love. Depending upon our own history which establishes enough basic trust to allow development in this area, we find ourselves needing to receive and to give affection in various ways.

Because the interpersonal needs are often significant issues and areas of pain for ACoA, this will be expanded on later in this book. There are some needs of which a person in ministry ought to be especially aware. Any kind of ministry is ordinarily a way of meeting a need to nurture and in some way to take care of another. As long as we have self-awareness of our own needs to take care of someone, to maintain the good feelings which that creates inside us, as long as we are able to realize that we are taking care of ourselves as well as others, then hopefully we can avoid some of the blind spots of needing, lest, as one of our colleagues phrases it, "we do good against people." Very often a high need to nurture others is in fact a defense against our own need to be taken care of. We deny that need and that we want to have others listen to and do for us. To be unaware of our own neediness and hungriness for another's care and concern can propel us into frantic and unrequited bouts of a nurturance which not only can burn us out but also can blind us to the real needs of the other.

Another "need trap" for the minister is the need to do well, the need which allows our own sense of competency to get measured by another's response to our being with them. Because persons ordinarily change slowly and with tiny steps that travel a spiral rather than a linear path, if we measure our own competency by another's quantum leaps, we are bound to be frustrated. All that we need to do with others is to be with them in an actively receptive way which allows each person to change and grow at his or her own rate.

The last need which someone in ministry might want to examine is the need to "do it right" (or "be right"). Unfortunately we are socialized by both our media and our religions that there is a "right," if not a "perfect" way to act or be. Our humanity is much more complex. Listening to and being with another is an art of presence, not a manual of technique. If we get too preoccupied with a need to do it right, we lose touch with ourselves, our God and whoever it is we may be trying to help.

The suggestions outlined above are invitational to the ongoing process of developing self-awareness. For the individual in ministry this process needs to be carefully tended through whatever means you find helpful. Support groups, personal therapy, individual or group, spiritual direction, working with dreams, using a personal journal, meditation—these are some of the paths you might choose to enhance your self-awareness so that the "you" that you bring to ministry is as free and available as possible.

Chapter 4

Spiritual Self-Awareness

Decades of experience indicate that the most effective method for the healing of addictions and the co-dependence of those enmeshed with the addicted is the development of a vital spirituality. Thus for you who will minister to adult children from dysfunctional families an awareness of your own spiritual life and hopes, as well as blocks and fears, will be an important first step.

- What was God called in your family?
- Remember your own mother (or mother figure) and, as best you can, her relationship with God. What did she teach you about God? At what age? Why?
- Remember your father (or father figure) and his relationship with God. How was it in evidence?
- What role did God have in your family? When was God remembered? When forgotten?
- How did God seem to you when you were small? Were there turning points in your relationship with God? Be specific in your memories as you chart (hopefully in a journal) your own salvation history.
- When, why, how did Jesus enter in on your spiritual journey? When, why, how did you discover the Holy Spirit?
- Journal for a while (and let your pen lead you from "out of the depths." Often this technique reveals more than your conscious and controlling memory can recall) about who God is for you right now. How do you image God? How do you draw God, dance God, sing God, touch God? What do you name God? What feelings about God are arising in you right now? How does God image you, name you? Listen.
- How do you image Jesus? Where is he? How is he? How do you feel about him? Have your feelings fluctuated over the years? What do you want from Jesus now?

41

- How do you image the Holy Spirit? What role has the Spirit in your life and ministry?
- What feels burned out, dead in your life, your ministry? What annoys you, even enrages you? What are you afraid of, what do you enjoy, what do you avoid in your life and ministry?
- What keeps you in ministry? Where do you find energy, peace and joy?
- Where do you find God/Jesus/Spirit in your day to day living?

If the ACoA to whom you minister are not yet aware of their pain or are not yet ready for recovery, they may not question the depths of your own spiritual life. Those, however, in the Twelve Step program gradually become alert to the spiritual dynamics in their healing process. There is surely, as AA notes, a distinction between spirituality and religion. Ministers represent religion in a public way. Hopefully we also are aware enough of and comfortable enough with our own spiritual life to serve as companion to those whose hope for healing includes, often centers on, the spiritual. In order, then, to minister to those using any Twelve Step program (AA, Al-Anon, ACoA, Overeaters Anonymous, etc.) we will be challenged to put down even deeper roots in our relationship with God.

The AA program and others based on it are spiritual at the core. The third step of the Twelve Steps is the turning of the recovering person's will, one's entire life over to one's higher power. In the third step the recovering person invites God, however each person images and names God, to change his or her mind and heart. In the eleventh step he or she pledges to seek a lifelong deepening of the relationship with God. To be involved with someone in recovery, someone who is really "working the program," presupposes that we ministers know how to tap deep wells of spiritual nourishment, not only in the ecclesial tradition, but within ourselves. Recovering addicts and co-dependents tend to be brutally honest with themselves, and will undoubtedly bring that honesty to bear in any relationship with a minister. If we ourselves are not seeking a lifelong deepening of our relationship with God, we will probably be found out.

How can the minister develop or deepen an awareness of the currents of the Spirit moving through not only ministerial activity but the humdrum of daily events? How can the minister develop a spiritual self-awareness? You have begun with some remembering and journaling. The most helpful ecclesial instrument of healing for the ACoA is the minister who knows, loves, speaks for and embodies the higher power. You are that ecclesial instrument of healing, no matter how shallow, sinful, inadequate you feel. You are the one to whom God has led the ACoA. In your very weakness, and honest acceptance of it, lies God's strength (2 Cor 12:9–10). In your ministry you will probably learn, grow, deepen your dependence on God's power. Walking with someone in a healing relationship will undoubtedly nourish your own spiritual life.

One Who Knows

There is a way in which adult children of alcoholics hit bottom. One of their crises at this point may be a loss of belief in God as God was taught and/or imbibed in their family of origin, or in the organized religion in which they were raised. Ministers do not need to defend God, the faith or the church from such a collapse. God often strips those "hitting bottom" of false gods. For example, some ACoA have made their co-dependent, "saintly" parent into "God." Hitting bottom for them may occur when life events all conspire to demythologize, de-idolize this false parental "God."

A minister who wants to serve such a person has begun to strip away from his or her own relationship with God some doctrinal decrees and pious platitudes. Such a minister has discovered God as alive, active and personally involved in healing. Such a minister has been claimed by Christ (Phil 3:12).

Thus, we ministers, perhaps through our own bottoming out in a crisis of faith or friendship, through loss of a parent or loss of meaning, know in our bones that Jesus lives, works, loves, heals. This knowing is not logically proving the existence of God or the resurrection of Jesus. This is the Jewish experience of knowing God and the one sent (Jn 17:3) which is life, relationship, union. A minister who knows God is growing in a most personal, most intimate relationship with God.

■ Reflect on what you know about God. Who taught you about God when you were younger? How did you learn? Why did you learn (since millions of children are taught but you were so deeply influenced by that teaching)? Who helps you know God now? How does that learning happen?

■ What pious platitudes have you let go of? Why? What do you *really* believe now about God/Jesus/Spirit? For what would you be willing to die?

■ When were you claimed by Christ? How does he keep hold of you? How do you feel about his claiming you?
■ How has your knowing God been nourished by those you minister with and to?

One Who Loves

A minister, surely, loves the Lord God with all his or her heart, mind, strength. It may be the puritan culture of the United States, it may be that many of us are from dysfunctional homes, but loving God/Jesus/Spirit is often a well kept and very individual secret. The Roman Catholic theologian Karl Rahner, noted for his splendid intellect, urges his readers to "throw your arms around Jesus."

■ Reflect on that last sentence. How does it make you feel? Surely Rahner does not mean male ministers? Surely not public demonstrations of affection? Surely good works are enough to indicate our love for God?

   If ministers must reexamine *who* it is we know, we must reexamine our fears of love, affection, intimacy with God.
■ On a scale of one to ten rank your freedom to be yourself with God:

1	5	10

great
guardedness

great
spontaneity

How do you feel about where you placed yourself? How did this "rank" happen in your life? If it is difficult to remember, ask the Spirit of truth to call some specific incidents to mind.
■ If you did not rank yourself a perfect 10, are there certain areas of your life and ministry which you do not want to share with God? Can you name them concretely? What feelings accompany your naming these areas?
■ How does God feel about your guarded areas? If you are not sure, ask; then sit quietly and listen. Perhaps journaling will release some hidden insights or buried feelings. Perhaps tonight or next week a dream will reveal some experiences or feelings which you guard from even yourself.

If our images of God fluctuate between dictator-judge and kind friend our devotion too may ebb and flow. Our affection may be blocked by anger with God's powerlessness. Our fears of what God might ask of us (some will read: require, demand of us) may overwhelm us. One way to explore our fear or embarrassment about loving God is to explore the freedom, spontaneity, playfulness with which we love some of our favorite human beings.

■ Whom do you currently love best in all the world? Think of that person in concrete detail and let your feeling for that person arise. Do you feel afraid? embarrassed? guarded? Why or why not?

■ On a scale of 1–10 rank your freedom to be yourself with your dearest person. How do you feel about where you placed yourself? How did this "rank" happen in your life? If it is difficult to remember, ask the Spirit of truth to call some specific incidents to mind.

■ If you did not rank yourself a perfect 10, are there certain areas of your life and ministry which you do not want to share with your dearest person? Can you name them concretely? What feelings accompany your naming these areas?

In Jesus, God has bridged that transcendent distance between us and God, a distance which *we* might feel more comfortable keeping. Jesus' own affection for God was obvious and attractive. Jesus' affection for such a variety of human beings puts flesh on God's affection for us. Our spirituality is simply our day to day response to this affection, God's "first loving us" (1 Jn 4:10).

One Who Speaks For

All the baptized continue Christ's ministry as prophet. Jesus challenged the self-satisfied and comforted the broken-hearted with his word. Prophets are so united with God that they, like Jesus, dare to speak on God's behalf, a word of critique, a word of consolation. Through them, God can channel a word to the community.

In a public way, we ministers are to hear the word of God, ponder it in our hearts, and speak it after discerning the appropriate moment. Listening to God's own concern for the adult child, still abused and oppressed by chains of the past, we can be gifted with a "word of consolation in the morning" (Is 50:4). This word of consolation is a gift from God. It may be honed by readings, courses and ongoing supervision in our ministry, but it is fundamentally God's to give, ours to beg for. This prophetic word is powerful and effective, penetrating to the joints and marrow of the human spirit (Heb 4:12). It will, of course, first penetrate to the depths of our own ministry and personal life.

- How do you best listen to God? Where? When?
- "The God of all consolation consoles us in all our afflictions" (2 Cor 1:3–4). Has that been true for you? Who "speaks" a consoling word to you? Remember specific incidents.
- When or how has the word of God penetrated to the "joints and marrow" of your ministry? Did the word comfort? critique? lay something bare? How deeply do you want the word to penetrate you?

Spiritual self-awareness means that we do want to grow more transparent to the word of God, letting God listen and speak through our listening heart. Sometimes God's word, however, is one of silent compassion, an empathy which does not need vocalization. It is clarity, our transparency to God, which communicates as we more and more decrease so that God's communication may more and more increase (Jn 3:30), that God's word may heal.

One Who Embodies

Have this mind in you which was also in Christ Jesus who did not consider being equal to God a thing to be clung to, but who emptied himself, taking the form of a slave . . . (Phil 2:5–7).

Hopefully, we do not consider being chosen by God something to be clung to. Hopefully we empty ourselves, taking on more solidarity with those suffering, as servants. Gradually, then, it is no longer we who live but Christ lives and loves and ministers in and through us (Gal 2:20).

The word of God continues to take flesh in our flesh; the incarnation continues. Jesus is not dead and gone, not far away on some starry throne, but within us, shaping us as we turn over our lives and ministries to him, shaping us into more effective instruments of healing. "Let them look up and see no longer me but only Jesus," John Henry Cardinal Newman prayed. We are the convincing sign of God's love made flesh for ACoA who have had such difficulty trusting any love, any supposed fidelity. Probably nothing will so effectively serve to heal their ruptured trust as loved ones and ministers who can embody the unconditional love and consistent fidelity of God.

Growing in Prayer

In being with adults who have been so severely damaged, our own authentic spiritual groundedness may prove even more therapeutic than psychological expertise. Many ministers confess, however, that they feel like impostors. They cry, "But I don't pray. How can I claim a spiritual life without this discipline?"

Prayer is not a discipline but a response to God's self-communication through the events and relationships of day to day living, a response to God's love. Our response may be silent or spoken, intercession or gratitude, laughter or groaning. It may be active in kindness and care, for "the least of the brothers and sisters" (Mt 25:40). It may be emotional response to a variety of stimuli, which emotions are openly laid before God for discernment, pruning, healing, strengthening. It may be the steady search to find God in all things, to learn (*discipulus/a*) God's love through every situation. Prayer cannot be boxed into devotions or a meditation period. When we protest that we cannot, will not or do not pray, an examination of where our hearts return at moments of mental rest indicates that there is more prayer/response to God than this world dreams of!

From this personal attachment of the heart flows our public presentation of God in preaching, teaching and communal prayer. Public expression of faith, leadership of the community in spiritual development, unabashed and joyful witness to God's love may be the first and most attractive sign to the ACoA that he or she will be listened to and understood. If we ministers—including those who do not use the pulpit, such as religious educators, youth ministers, visitors of the shut-ins, etc.—communicate God, God who invites healing, the ACoA in our community may begin to trust us as an instrument of that healing.

St. Paul says that he doesn't even bother to judge his own progress but leaves that to the Lord. We too can leave spiritual pulse-taking to God and offer ourselves with as much spiritual authenticity as possible as companions on the ACoA's journey toward healing. We need not look pious, pray profusely, preach eloquently but simply be aware of our own journey to God, our own journey in grace. To be real with a God who is real, inviting us to a real and ever-increasingly intimate relationship, and to share our God and ourselves with others is a most effective ministry to ACoA—and everyone.

Conclusion

As you finish, for now, exploring your self-awareness in its psychological and spiritual development, you may be very aware that you grew up in an alcohol-centered home or in a family in which some other parental sickness or absence has left deep, perhaps still unhealed wounds. If you know or even suspect that your family of origin was/is dysfunctional, we recommend more exercises in spiritual and psychological self-reflection.

For personal reflection, both Claudia Black's workbook, *Repeat After Me* (Denver: MAC, 1985) and Patti McConnell's (pseud.) *A Workbook for Healing: Adult Children of Alcoholics* (San Francisco: Harper and Row, 1986) are very helpful. McConnell's final chapters on forgiveness highlight so well a core gift of Christ to his community. Combining personal reflection on emotional and relational history with spiritual exercises for deepening one's relationship with God/Jesus/Spirit, *Hope for Healing: Good News for Adult Children of Alcoholics* (Callahan and McDonnell, Mahwah, N.J.: Paulist, 1987) continues and focuses some of the self-awareness reflections which you have just completed in this book.

Chapter 5

When the Minister
Is an Adult Child

This last chapter in Part II will focus on raising a particular self-awareness when the minister is an adult child.

Statistically at least, there is a good chance that you are the adult child of a dysfunctional family or an ACoA. While there are no definitive statistics which identify the numbers of persons in ministry who grew up in dysfunctional families, we can assume that the number in ministerial and helping professions is at least as high as the general population. David Treadway, Ph.D., writer and lecturer in the field of families and substance abuse, estimates that the number of ACoA in his training audiences are eighty percent.[1] Virginia Satir, family theorist and therapist, places the number of dysfunctional families as high as ninety-five percent.[2] (Of course, the range of dysfunction is from moderate to severe.)

In order to enhance your self-awareness this chapter will attempt to describe very simply the phenomena of transference and countertransference, and some of the possible vulnerabilities which the minister as adult child may carry in these areas. It will also describe some of the commonly held assumptions about ministry which might "hook" the ACoA. As in the previous chapters, you will be invited to take some time and space for prayerful reflection.

Our personal history impacts the way in which we work both with individuals and as members of a team. Our history impacts our experience of authority and how we function in either a supervisory or supervisee role. As persons in ministry our role as well as our personal characteristics will evoke certain responses from the persons with whom we work. In order to understand this we need to appreciate the power of the phenomena of transference and countertransference.

The concept of transference developed in the early psychoanalytic movement when Sigmund Freud discovered that patients often "transferred" onto him the powerful feelings, both positive and nega-tive, which they had experienced toward earlier parental figures. In-deed, the core of analytic therapy consisted in the working through of transference. Anyone who has been engaged in any long-term inten-sive psychotherapeutic work knows from experience the extraordi-nary potency of transferential feeling. All the feelings of childhood, love, hate, dependency, anger, fear, can get reexperienced, with the therapist becoming the focus of past feelings toward parents.

Very often persons who represent the church become the recipi-ents of a person's feelings about parents and authority. To be the recipient of these feelings in a non-threatened and a non-exploitative way demands an ongoing attentiveness to our own processes of fam-ily and self-awareness.

Ministry also requires that we are sensitive to countertransfer-ence issues. Each of us brings into every helping relationship not only our own current needs, values, and expectations, but also all of our past experiences. Countertransference refers to the feelings from our own history which are apt to get triggered in working with other people.

■ Can you name the kinds of people and issues that you know you are "allergic" to?

—persons who are actively abusing
  spouse or children?
  drugs?
  alcohol?
—explosive anger?
—clingy dependency?
—domineering?

■ Who are the kinds of people and what are the kinds of issues which you think might lure you into extra care-taking and/or rescu-ing efforts from you?

—the "waif"?
—helplessness?
—crisis?

■ Do you have a need

—to do ministry perfectly?
—to do it right?
—to be right?

—to do good?
—to be liked by the persons with whom you work?
—by *all* those persons?

As with all of these exercises of self-awareness let yourself be with them gently and with an acceptance of the reality of what you are today.

Assumptions About Ministry

Some of the commonly held assumptions about ministry have been reinforced by treating some particular sayings in the gospels with a concrete literalism. The historical-critical methodology used by scripture scholars during the past ninety years is much appreciated by ministers. Yet after centuries of attributing literally to Jesus many specific sayings, popular faith may have contributed to unreal assumptions about ministry. Since the assumptions get reinforced by the expectations of many persons to whom you minister it is important to be able to name them and to discern your response.

Assumption 1.   Ministers should be totally available.

"Feed my lambs . . ."

The issue of discerning appropriate boundaries and limits is an ongoing challenge for persons in ministry. How do we respond to the limitless needs? In some ministry settings there are neither the boundaries of office hours nor rotation of shifts. In some ministry settings the minister is expected to be available not only at all hours but also to all kinds of constituencies. He or she may live and work in the same building as well.

The "hook" for the minister who is an adult child is the issue of boundaries and limits. Especially if you were the responsible child in your own family, responsible either for some of the material well-being (for example, cooking the meals, keeping the house) or for the emotional climate (for example, keeping the peace or creating distraction from the family dysfunction) you are probably vulnerable in this area. As a minister attempting to become more responsive and responsible to the gospel, you probably also yearn to *be* and *do* as much as you are able to communicate the good news. So the task of discerning your own personal balance of zeal and workaholism is a delicate one. Sometimes our bodies give us some clues about where the balance lies. Illness, persistent fatigue, mental stress are signals which deserve attention. Our own patterns of vulnerability to sin, particularly those patterns with a rhythm which matches our level of overwork, for example, irascibility, taking our irritations out on the persons we love, might offer us clues in the delicate discernment between zeal and workaholism.

Take some time and invite the Spirit of truth to show you your own truth.

■ How much do you believe that ministers should be totally available?

■ What are the "boundaries" in your own ministry setting?

—time?
—space?
—delegation of responsibility?

■ What are the signals you need to be aware of which might flag overwork?

—tension? muscular or mental?
—fatigue?
—isolation from peers?
—patterns of sinfulness?

Ask the Spirit to keep on revealing ways which can free you to become a more effective minister of the good news:

—taking space and time for prayer, reflection, study, exercise, recreation.
—keeping a balance of good diet, rest, work.

Assumption 2. The person in ministry is expected to make an almost total donation of self.

"Deny yourself . . ."

Whether this takes the form of a co-dependent "de-selfing" or whether it takes the form of an overidentification with the formal role and/or organization of church ministry, this assumption about ministry can be harmful. "De-selfing"[3] is a central characteristic of co-dependency. Who I am is defined by who someone else is. For example, a favorite co-dependent joke is:

Q. What flashes before a co-dependent's eyes when he or she is going to die?

A. Someone else's life.[4]

There are ways in which a minister can subtly or not so subtly get drawn into an unhealthy style of being for others. Often within the church as organization this behavior is formally or informally rewarded. Certainly within hierarchical systems it is the "company person" who usually advances.

A critical discernment question for anyone in ministry is the sifting of behavior and motivation which is co-dependent without a running away from the heart of Christianity, loving the other as ourself.

The adult child is pre-disposed by his or her history to co-dependence. The early experiences of inconsistent and conditional parental affection and approval often generate negative self-esteem and an inordinate reliance on the affirmation of others. Growing up in an environment which demands a fairly rigid compliance with certain rules and roles, there is little opportunity for the normal development of a true sense of self. The ACoA in ministry can be tempted into the self-definition of others' perceived needs and others' approval. We may solidify a rigid compliance with certain rules and roles. Sometimes we may need to create needs in others in order to keep at bay old guilts and fears. A good way to identify whether this is a personal pattern is to look for the following sequence in our helping relationship.[5]

Rescuer: Do I leap in to help, even when I may neither be asked nor really needed?

Persecutor: Do I find myself blaming the person(s) whom I rescue?

Victim: Do I often feel put upon or unappreciated?

The rescuer eventually becomes the blaming persecutor and finally falls into a victim stance because "no one appreciates me"—until the next rescue opportunity when the cycle begins again.

The adult child is more adept at nurturing than at receiving nurturance. What looks to all like an unreserved donation of self can in fact be a defense against our own neediness and fear of abandonment/rejection. The best defense against needing others for support and nurture is to deny these needs and take on the role of taking care of others, even when they neither want nor need the care.

A variant of an exercise described by Anthony De Mello[6] might be helpful in your discernment of the practical differences between co-dependent love and Christian love.

■ Take some time to let yourself become quiet and centered. Imagine Jesus looking at you lovingly and tenderly. Take as much time as you need in letting yourself be nurtured by this loving and compassionate look of Jesus. He knows from the inside what it means to be human. After you have spent some time letting Jesus look at you with tenderness and unconditional acceptance, ask the Spirit of truth to let you see whose needs you are serving in your ministry. Ask for the grace to recognize co-dependency and, just for today, to surrender it.

Assumption 3.   The person in ministry is expected to be better than others, to be perfect.

"Be you perfect . . ."

Society has certain expectations of persons in ministry which go beyond expectations of the ordinary persons who each of us in ministry is. A person in public leadership (be that church or public office) makes headlines whenever scandal or sin (especially sexual sin) becomes known. There is a legitimacy about accountability to a public trust. Sometimes, however, this gets confused with a larger-than-life requirement to be perfect. The adult child, who has not had much experience of "normal," is vulnerable to an enormous amount of tension between the poles of perfectionism and an intense self-criticism.

The requirement for perfection also can get tangled with two other issues which adult children frequently struggle with: control and boundaries. Both show up in difficulties with team ministry. An excessive need for control makes it difficult to have the collegiality and subsidiarity which is required in effective team ministry. Over-involvement in details which would more appropriately be delegated might (up to a point) allow them to be done according to my requirements for perfection. This lack of trust in any standards short of perfection does not enhance team spirit.

Sometimes when the adult child is in a supervisory capacity his or her perfectionism shows up in an excessive demand for compliance. Because boundary issues are not clear, we then sometimes think that the performance of the person to whom we delegate reflects inordinately upon ourselves. Good delegation lets go not only of authority but also of responsibility.

The core issue of perfectionism is the issue of human limits. Both the need for perfection and the need for control are centrally about the reality that God is God and we are creatures. This robust principle and foundation of St. Ignatius Loyola's spirituality is at the heart, too, of the Twelve Step philosophy and program. The acceptance of our own limits facilitates realistic self-acceptance, self-forgiveness and a realistic view of our own potency for changing ourselves and certain circumstances. Eventually this leads to the acceptance and finally forgiveness which is part of the recovery process.

■ Thus, the last reflection in this section will be the invitation to spend some time with the Serenity Prayer of the Twelve Step program:

> God, grant me the serenity (the trust) to accept those things I cannot change; the courage (the truth, vision, zeal) to change those things I can; and the wisdom to know the difference.

PART III

The Ministry—Public Leadership

Some Christian denominations have always valued the lay evangelist, the lay preacher. In some parts of the world and now even in North America, other denominations must rely on lay leadership in the liturgical assembly due to a shortage of ordained clergy. Thus, we do not mean to exclude the non-ordained in this section on public leadership. Surely many laity minister as teachers, catechists, preachers of retreats, leaders of Bible study for adults, teens and children. In these areas of public leadership, the awareness and healing of adult children can be facilitated by the alert and sensitive minister who serves as liturgical leader, preacher or teacher.

Chapter 6

Liturgical Leadership

Often the first contact a parishioner has with a minister is at the Sunday service. If long term healing is to begin it may well start with a worship service. Before the presider begins to preach, however, the demeanor, inner peace and inner authority of the leader will have an impact on the ACoA.

The presider at the liturgy often represents in the participants' minds the only priest, Christ, who stands before God making intercession for us (Heb 7:25). The minister not only embodies Christ making intercession, but he or she often models and is a conduit for God's graciousness to the congregation, God's hospitality. Whereas all other forms of ministry are shared among the congregation, including some of the functions of the liturgical leader, it is as presider that the ordained most often serve.

Ordination does not confer power, although some ordained still operate with a power, rather than a service, orientation. Ordination is the juridical appointment of those who give evidence of God's gift, the gift of ordering all the various gifts of the community. Ignatius of Antioch likens the bishop (bishops were the first ones ordained in church history) to a conductor of an orchestra, drawing all the instruments and notes together in harmony. Today the image might apply to the local pastor as well.

As president of the assembly at worship, the presider has enormous mythic power to help the stories and symbols of the tradition live or wither away Sunday after Sunday. Whether extrovert or introvert, the leader of prayer needs only to be authentic in his or her greeting, prayer, intercession, offering, and thanksgiving.

ACoA are particularly sensitive to inauthenticity, having lived with so much of it. A presider whose sullenness bespeaks an inability to relate either to God or to people, or whose "joy" is so superficial, merely pasted on for the occasion, can lead ACoA to wonder who then can relate to God. Presiders who pray from their own hearts as well as from liturgical texts, yet not merely reciting words, are attractive to ACoA, even if the prayers are not erudite or eloquent. St. Paul himself was not eloquent, but he would boast of his weakness, for when he was most weak, then God's power in him was most strong (Rom 8:26; 2 Cor 12:10).

For the presider who is an ACoA, authenticity is also key. He or she may be engrained in the role, wearing a mask of piety. As such a minister begins to heal, his or her liturgical style will undoubtedly flex, simplify, move from self-preoccupation to a deepening focus on God's action in public worship.

Chapter 7

Preaching

One of the major functions of the ordained minister is preaching. Since that medium brings the preacher into contact with the widest spectrum of parishioners, it is undoubtedly an important opportunity for most people to hear the good news of hope for their healing. "How can they believe if there is no one to preach the word?" asks St. Paul (Rom 10:4). With so many individuals and families tortured by the bad news of growing up in a diseased family, what belief can the preacher encourage?

The New Testament offers an effective model for preaching. The proclamation of good news always precedes exhortation. If in the short-hand of the New Testament it sometimes seems that proclamation and exhortation occur in the same sermon, in our day the proclamation of *good* news might have to take center stage for years in our churches, because many of us can barely believe it. Until the congregation has grasped how well loved by God it is, how saved from hopelessness by Jesus it is, how dignified through the indwelling and action of the Spirit it is, the community is not told how to act, behave, perform. ACoA ears may have been so dulled by an abusive home situation that only years of hearing the proclamation of God's love embodied in Jesus and poured into our hearts by the Holy Spirit (Rom 5:5) will begin to heal the bad news which adult children think they are.

Our own ears as ministers may have been dulled, too, by preachers and other religious authorities who have projected onto God the tyranny which they themselves experienced in their own upbringing. Their sermons and doctrines which we may have absorbed in our youth were not exhortation and encouragement in responding to God's love. Rather, they may have moralized and harangued the very people whose hunger for God led them to worship services in the first place. Just as ACoA who are not aware, not in the process of recovery, hand on to their children a distorted parenting, so religious leaders not in touch with the fear, rigidity, legalism

61

and/or need for power which governs their "leadership" only compound the suffering of those who trust them. This is bad news.

Good news however sets free. When parishioners find a home in the word of God, as Jesus in John's gospel urges them to do, they become disciples, learners; they know the truth and that truth sets free. "Make my word your home and you will be my disciples (*discipulus/a:* learner, pupil); you will know the truth and the truth will set you free" (Jn 8:32).

Ministers, ordained or lay, are those gifted in helping people find a home in the good news, *the* word of Christ. Christ will make disciples, teach truth and set free.

Preachers especially, in explaining and interpreting the gospel, can introduce the congregation Sunday after Sunday to the living Christ Jesus made so accessible. Gospels are not biographies of Jesus but invitations for every hearer of the good news to become engaged with Jesus, participate in his living and loving, share his dying and rising, grow in intimacy with him. Gospels are invitations to know Jesus, and if knowing him is eternal life (Jn 17:3) it is because knowing another means loving union with that other. To know Jesus means to love him in a deep, vulnerable, intimate sharing of life together. Gospels help us know, not about Jesus, but to know him directly.

Hearers of the good news need from their ministers not so much a fascinating exegetical detail, nor a retelling of the pericope. They need a graphic, sensual, imaginative depiction of what Jesus is doing in his relationship with the ordinary walking wounded of his day. They need to know that when the gospel is proclaimed, Jesus, alive in their midst, continues today his action of healing, comforting, welcoming sinners and outcasts, confronting those who lay heavy burdens on other people's backs. Jesus' action lives today in his body, his church, his people. It is not Zacchaeus whom Jesus wants to eat with in the twentieth century but Debbie and Nick and Pat. In that story, Jesus who is alive and well and active, cries out "Debbie (or Nick or Pat or ———), come here! I want to eat with you today."

Scripture is a sacrament. It effects what it signifies, it does what it says. If God says through the prophet Ezekiel that God is a good shepherd searching for the lost, bandaging the hurt, feeding the hungry and setting the strong and healthy out to play (Ez 34:15–16), then as we hear this good news, God is doing that *now* to those in our congregation who are lost, hurt, hungry or healthy. God is doing that now within each of us, too, tending those parts of our lives which feel lost, hurt, hungry or healthy.

Usually the preacher first proclaims the gospel to the congregation. When we hear the story of Jesus healing the blind man proclaimed, because Jesus lives and works on our behalf, and because scripture is itself a power-full sacrament, some of our blindness is being healed as we hear/read/ponder. When Jesus raises the widow's son, he raises some dead part of us to new life. When Jesus touches a paralytic, our crippled hearts can move more freely. Scripture effects what it signifies, does what it says. This word is a living, life-giving word which penetrates gradually but deeply like rain penetrating the earth. It does not return to God empty but accomplishes that for which it is sent: our fruitfulness (Is 55:10–11). Being at home with and in this word sets free.

Preaching, too, is a sacrament, a way in which God can communicate grace, God's own abundant life, through a very human medium. Bread, wine, water, oil are visible, tangible instruments of God's grace—and how much more the person and powerful word of the minister who hands on the good news of God's love poured into our hearts!

By the way they proclaim good news and preach the gospel's message of love and healing, preachers can do much to facilitate God's restoring hope and trust in the hearts of those so betrayed in their youth. Preachers may occasionally want to let the word "lay bare the thoughts and motives of the heart" (Heb 4:12) and treat the need for healing directly.

An Example

For example, after proclaiming the pericope of the paralyzed man lifted to the roof and then lowered by four friends, you might openly remind the congregation that some painful incidents or an entire childhood filled with cruelty, abuse, neglect, inconsistency may have traumatized various ones of us or various parts of our lives. In some aspects we are just as paralyzed as the man on the pallet. Ask the congregation to remember such an incident or whole years and decades when they felt so tightly bound, so emotionally frozen, so spiritually paralyzed. Give them some silent time to remember (of course, some will resent this exercise, for if you keep talking from the pulpit they can continue to keep dulling their ears, minds, and hearts).

Then ask them to remember four friends, relatives, loved ones who did, would or could bring them to Jesus. Not four can be found? Maybe two? One? No one? (Realistically, in a given congregation there are those so depressed and/or damaged that they feel utterly alone and uncared for.) Invite those with friends to image themselves being lifted to the rooftop. What feelings arise? What happens to trust?

Then "leave the ninety-nine" and turn again to the ones who feel so deprived of friends, so alone; invite them to change the gospel story. Invite them to imagine themselves lying paralyzed, on the ground in the house next door to the house where Jesus is teaching. Although he has no time to eat because of the crowd, imagine him tapping Peter's shoulder, saying, "Get me through this crowd, Peter. I have someone who needs me." Watch Peter bulldoze through the crowd, officiously crying: "Make way, make way!"

Jesus blinks in the sunlight. You can see him through your open door. He turns, as though looking for someone. He sees you and walks directly through your door. His hand rests on your arm as he crouches down next to you. He asks you to talk to him, to tell him how you feel, to cry bitterly, angrily, to weep sorrowfully because you feel so abandoned. He listens, and as he does, he strokes your arm, kneads your shoulder muscles, brushes your hair off your forehead.

Invite these lonely ones in your congregation to finish this exercise at home. Call the befriended ones back from their imaginative interactions with their own paralysis, their own friends and Jesus. Invite all of them to take time *today* to finish showing Jesus their wounds, their feelings, their desire for healing and freedom and friends. *Today*, in the liturgy of the whole church around the world, Jesus stands alive, ready and eager to heal whatever is unfree, paralyzed, unbefriended in our persons, our relationships, our lives. *Today*, as we finish our eucharistic celebration together, we invite our congregation to give Jesus our priest all the past pain and to join him in his dying and rising.

Further examples of using this immediacy of the gospel, this contemporaneity with Jesus (Kierkegaard), this gospel contemplation (Ignatius Loyola) may be found in *Hope for Healing: Good News for Adult Children of Alcoholics*. There are exercises which flow from stories of Jesus' healing of the leper (Mk 1:40–45);[1] his straightening the back of the woman bent for eighteen years (Lk 13:10–17);[2] Jesus' blessing the children (Mt 19:13–15);[3] and more (Mk 5:25–34, the woman with the twelve year hemorrhage; Mk 5:1–17, the demon-possessed man who cut himself with rocks; Lk 7:36–50, the sinful woman who wept and washed Jesus' feet).[4] With a bit of imagination by the preacher these exercises can be transformed from helps for personal prayer to invitations to a congregation to let Jesus heal their hearts.

In the lectionaries of major denominations, many healing, feeding and exorcising actions of Jesus are proclaimed Sunday after Sunday, year after year. In the proclamation, through the sermon, Jesus comes again to work in our congregations. Because these gospel events are a living word, even were we to preach the pericope of the paralyzed man every year, the word has a life of its own. The hearers are interiorly different this year from last. They are more open or more closed to good news, more healed or more hurt, more fearful or more hopeful. They bring themselves just as they are to this living word proclaimed. They begin to find a home in it, in Christ, and he can set them more free Sunday after Sunday, year after year.

Preaching God

One of the areas in which Jesus sets free is our understanding of God. Although the reworking of images of God happens through spiritual direction as God becomes more real, preaching which is Christ-centered, gospel oriented, can also help the congregation discover anew who God is.

Jesus calls God "Father," and during his agony in the garden, Mark's gospel reports that he called God "Abba" or Daddy (Mk 14:36). That privileged title expressing a unique relationship has led many Christians to believe that God is, in essence, Father. However, there is no way we can ever limit God to being just Father. God is so much more than Father, more than mother, more than parent. We cannot find words to express who God is because to name God is to define; to define means to place limits on, and that denies the God of freedom, mystery. God is more than we can say, dream of, imagine. Jesus himself said that God is like a father welcoming home the prodigal, but also that God is like a shepherd and that God is like a woman (Luke 15:1–32).

Muslims have one hundred names for God; Hindus recite one thousand. The Jewish scriptures abound in images, titles, descriptions of God: warrior, dew, seamstress, shield, nurse, rock, gardener, etc. God cannot be limited by our experience of God's mystery.

Sometimes adult children who have abusive fathers turn from God, fearing more abuse and rejection. Sometimes God becomes the good Father who makes up for an emotionally absent parent. Sometimes, if the father is co-dependent, all the sweet but sick ways a co-dependent dad relates to spouse, children and world get projected onto God. These people, then, cannot bear to read of God's anger in scripture or to see God as warrior on the side of the oppressed. Nor does it help an ACoA to substitute God as mother. Mother, whether alcoholic or co-dependent, was also sick.

Preachers can help break parishioners out of absolutizing any title or role for God. They can preach, according to the scriptures of the Sunday, about God as so much more than parent. They can especially point to the one who best embodies God—Jesus, the image of God (Heb 1:3). The word of God takes flesh so that we can see, hear, touch God (1 Jn 1:1). If God was trying to communicate who God is, what God wants for so many centuries, God finally, definitively, spoke all that God is in Jesus (Heb 1:1–2). If we want to see God, Jesus tells Philip at the last supper, we are to look to him, Jesus (Jn 14:9).

"What response can we make to the Lord for all the good God has given?" (Ps 116:12). What response can we make to the gift of God's own self given us in Jesus? Only after the proclamation of good news comes the exhortation. Many sermons unfortunately, focus only on our behavior, how we *should* act, much of which reinforces unhealthy rules handed down by dysfunctional parents or society. Chances are that the ACoA who still come to worship on Sundays, for example, were brought up afraid to trust themselves, their feelings, thoughts, desires. In order not to make the chaos at home any worse, they practiced "perfection" and projected that demand for perfection onto God. Undoubtedly they heard that exhortation to be perfect regularly from the pulpit as well. How can preachers, once the good news of Christ's love has begun to sink in, exhort their congregations to respond in healthy ways?

If for the Jews the way to respond to God's love was to keep the law, Torah, we Christians may have been taught to do God's will, to follow Christ, or to be perfect. We hardly have heard from preacher or teacher Paul's ringing words about our freedom from law, our salvation already won by Christ, the Spirit who dwells within us. Jesus railed against legalistic Pharisees who thwarted the true expression of the Torah by placing heavy burdens on already bent backs. Some of our church authorities—hopefully unwittingly—may be burdening today's Christians, feeding into the psycho-spiritual damage which they suffered in dysfunctional homes. Let us explore how preachers (or teachers) might rework just four concepts which may tyrannize adult children today: perfection, following Christ (discipleship and discipline), "God's holy will," and love.

Perfection

"Be perfect as your heavenly Father is perfect" (Mt 5:48). What does perfect mean, one teacher challenges her adult students. Whether they are ACoA or not, most of them respond:

- not showing weakness, feelings, bad manners, etc.
- not making mistakes, bad grades, an error on the ball field, etc.
- not breaking any laws of the land or family taboos, cultural customs or religious rules, etc.
- but being proper, courteous, angelic, virtuous, serene, etc.

This is the epitome of impression-management, a prime characteristic of the co-dependent. This is the antithesis of being who we are, as God made us, for God's glory: human beings fully alive. This message from home is sometimes reinforced from the pulpit. It is almost as though this one injunction "sums up the law and the prophets."

There must be something perverse in us Christians which keeps us so focused on achieving our own perfection (whatever that is) when the rest of the New Testament uses the passive verb: we *are* perfected, and not by our own doing but by the grace of God. Mark's gospel, the first written, proclaims the great commandment as loving God and neighbor *as* we love ourselves (Mk 12:28–33). John's gospel promotes love as the only commandment, loving *as* Jesus loves (Jn 13:34). Paul, who announces that Christ has set us free from the law, seems to understand the human craving for security and so allows that if we want to fulfill the law of Christ we can bear one another's burdens (Gal 6:2).

It is Luke, however, undoubtedly sharing much of Matthew's sermon material, who takes the exhortation to "perfection" and uses quite a different word. Most Christians when asked cannot fill in the blanks from Luke's good news: "Be you _____ as your heavenly Father is _____." Translations vary: compassionate, merciful, forgiving—*as* your Father is compassionate, letting rain (and blessing) fall on the good and bad alike. "Be you compassionate as your heavenly Father is compassionate" (Lk 6:36).

Note that compassion, unlike perfection, is relational. Note that we have scant idea of what God's "perfection" is like, but hopefully some lived experience of what God's compassion is like. God's perfection, Stoic philosophers taught, even before Christianity merged with it, was primarily *a-pathos.* God was *a* (without)–*pathos* (passion). This is far from the Jewish (thus Jesus') appreciation of God with a whole range of emotion: tenderness, anger, joy, rage, hatred, love; and a whole range of activity to express those emotions: dancing, destroying, shaping, sewing, planting, comforting, cuddling, carrying, feeding, uprooting, bandaging. Jesus' God was full of passion which is deep, long-lasting emotion. That is why God has compassion, shares our emotions with their range, depth and variety. God is with (*com*) us in our passion, which also means suffering.

Following Christ

Suffering, so many preachers have insisted, is the hallmark of the Christian. To ACoA ears, this is bad news. They already gave—and gave, and gave. Three statements from the synoptic gospels, invitations to discipleship, stand out. Paul does not allude to "following" Christ, and John has another interpretation of discipleship. We will examine the synoptics and John.

The classic call to discipleship, used in all three synoptic gospels, is: If you want to be my disciple, take up your cross and follow me (Mk 8:34, and parallels). The image is frightening: a lonely, isolated march, seeing only Jesus' back in the distance, dreading what one knows of the outcome; crucifixion, with all the other tortures which lead to Calvary; betrayal, arrest, abandonment, jail, scourging, crowning with thorns, ridicule, pain, thirst. For adult children, life has brought too much of that already, and so no wonder if they keep a distance from the cross-carrying Jesus. Yet ACoA, like all Christians, need to deepen their discipleship. The synoptic evangelists suggest two ways, and John another, quite different, understanding.

Most serious Christians—and ACoA who have stayed with the church tend to be very serious about their commitment—cringe at hearing Jesus say to the rich man: Go sell what you have, give to the poor, and come, follow me (Mk 10:21, and parallels). How many riches still burden them, they groan guiltily. Following is so costly. However, the words preceding Jesus' invitation are: "Jesus looked at the man tenderly, and said . . ." ACoA need to look at Jesus looking at them tenderly.

Perhaps for years they need to see Jesus looking at them tenderly. Then, gradually, slowly, perhaps over many years, the ego-hole which was created as youngsters by deficient parenting will begin to fill, heal. They will begin to believe they are loved, cherished, wanted, tenderly held by the loving eyes of Jesus. When that happens, other "things" which they stuffed into that gaping wound —alcohol, drugs, cigarettes, candy, money, computers, sleep, etc. —will gradually lose importance in their life. Like a good mother who looks on her infant tenderly,[5] Jesus will begin to be nourishment for the hungry heart. Jesus will gradually wean the ACoA (or anyone, for that matter) from whatever "riches" they thought they could not live without.

Some discipline themselves, structuring their lives so as to renounce material blessings, to control their joy in the good things of earth. That kind of discipline, always difficult and painful, poses as virtue. True discipline, however, is any disciple-making activity which deepens our relationship with Christ. Notice that discipline then is relational, flowing from our desire to be more closely allied with Jesus, and is quite distinct from the Stoic "perfection" of squelching our very human selves. Our efforts at detachment, self-sacrifice, "discipline" may well be a repression of our needs and desires. When the weaning process is in Jesus' control, however, we are truly set free.

Another call to discipleship includes Jesus' requirement of allegiance, "letting the dead bury the dead" (Mt 8:22). Many adult children hover around their living, still sick, parents hoping for a word of approval, a gesture of love. Their heart is divided between the love and work found in the present moment and the old longings from the past relationships with parents. Jesus' seeming harshness in this call to discipleship may, for adult children, be a call away from co-dependency to a life centered in the present, strengthened by his presence.

Finally, John's understanding of discipleship may well provide a healing alternative to the individual's isolated following in Christ's footsteps. For John, discipleship is not about following but about learning. A *discipulus/a* (Latin) is a learner, a student. Jesus is portrayed as learning from God because he is so close to the heart of God (Jn 1:18).

Heart-to-heart intimacy is what John's Jesus calls us to. The beloved disciple who leans against Jesus' heart at the last supper models that intimacy. He learns from Jesus, as do all the disciples: "I do not call you servants but friends because I have made known to you all that I have learned from my Father" (Jn 15:15).

There is no taking up *our* cross but there is, for the beloved disciple, a call to be with Jesus as he goes to *his* cross. The beloved disciple is not alone, but travels with Peter to the high priest's house, stands with Mary on Calvary, runs with Peter to see the empty tomb, fishes with Peter and recognizes the risen Christ. Discipleship according to this gospel means learning from the heart, being with, relating most intimately with Christ. That is good news.

The Will of God

How did it begin, this blaming the inexplicable pain and evil in the world on the "will of God"? How do "bad things happen to good people"? Was it the keepers of organized religion who perpetrated "the answer" to human suffering? Does it spring from a more ancient source, Mark's gospel, when during Jesus' agony in the garden he cries: "Not my will but thine be done" (Mk 14:36)? Then his torturers arrive, leaving us with the distinct and terrifying impression that Jesus' cruel and unjust execution is "God's holy will."

Theologians through the ages have divided God's will so neatly into active will, passive will, permissive will, etc. but the conclusion is inescapable, writes Rabbi Harold Kushner (whom some Christians tend to dismiss because he does not know the resurrection). Either God is all-powerful, or God is all-loving.[6] Kushner, and now others, Christians, suggest that perhaps all-powerful is not an attribute of God but a cultural bias in a patriarchal society which overvalues power.[7] To explore new appreciations of God's will we will focus on power, pain and freedom.

Power is ascribed to God continually in our liturgies. So many of our formal prayers begin: all-powerful or omnipotent or almighty God. AA groups and their offspring refer to the higher power. To hand over control of one's life to a higher power does provide true healing, and we have evidence. Yet divine power is often wrongly associated with magic or rescue rather than with its meaning in Greek, *dynamis*, energy. The higher energy which heals is indeed God's energy. Across cultures and centuries, the energy of life received heals and harmonizes. For example, the *Tao Te Ching* by China's ancient sage, Lao Tzu, describes a life process, a spirituality operating since the fifth century BCE, which taps into the divine energy in the universe.[8]

Rabbi Kushner opts for God as all-loving, Lao Tzu knows that all energy moves toward unity, but we Christians have our own way to understand God's power. We look to Jesus. If you want to see God, Jesus assures Philip, look to me (Jn 14:9). Jesus is a prophet, powerful in word and deed (Lk 24:19). We have equated his miracles with rescuing people from misery, but theologians note that other Jewish prophets and even Greek "divine men" could heal and even raise the dead. It may be more helpful to look at Jesus' "power" as love/energy flowing through him to restore health, wholeness and even life. We see Jesus using all his love and energy to war against suffering, injustice and pain. To know what God wills we look at what Jesus wills.

God hates pain. God's will and energy works to heal pain, fight injustice. How can we know? We look to Jesus. God's will, then, is not for Jesus to be betrayed, tortured and killed. If we change the cliché noun, "God's will," to a verb; "what God wants," or even an emotion-laden verb, "what God passionately desires," we can break out of a mind set that God even "permits," let alone "wills," human suffering. Just as Jesus wanted, passionately desired, healing, wholeness, love for people he encountered, so does God.

A passive God who "permits" smacks of the Stoic God who is *a-pathos* (note our word "apathy"). God passionately desires our human freedom. All the books of the Jewish scriptures sing of God's most "mighty deed," freeing a people from slavery in Egypt. Exodus freedom is a theme of Jewish writings and liturgies even today. God passionately desired freedom for Jesus and for all those who surrounded him during those fateful days: freedom for disciples who betrayed, slept, ran away; freedom for soldiers, high priests and Pilate.

"Freely I lay down my life," Jesus asserts (Jn 10:18). God would have continued loving Jesus had he walked out of Gethsemane and back to a secluded life in Nazareth. God's love for Jesus, like God's love for us, is not conditional upon our "works." God has missioned Jesus to preach the good news of God's abundant, unconditional love (*hesed*), and Jesus would be faithful to that vocation, no matter what the cost. To retract the good news would be to betray his God, the "little ones" of Israel and us today. And so, he "accepted the things he could not change"—his death—because he had spent his ministry with "courage to change the things" he could. He did not want crucifixion, God did not want his crucifixion, but both desired freedom, for Jesus and even for those who would abuse it.

God did not "need" the crucifixion of Jesus to save the world. Jesus did not need to redeem us from Satan and certainly did not need to buy off God's wrath. That kind of God, so often the one preached and taught, is a blood-thirsty tyrant sometimes used by parents, teachers and pastors to bolster their own lack of authority. That kind of God has tyrannized children and adults too long. That is the "eye-for-eye" God whom some might preach, while "laying heavy burdens on people's backs." The God of Jesus is best known through Jesus himself, and God's will is best found by looking at what Jesus himself willed, wanted, passionately desired.

Love

Jesus passionately desired that we be one. The conclusion of his prayer, "*as* the Father and I are one" (Jn 17:21), is crucial for ACoA. Jesus willed that we should love one another, but the conclusion "*as* I have loved you" (Jn 13:34) is crucial for adult children. Because ACoA are suffering from co-dependency, they need to reexamine "Christian love," so frequently encouraged from the pulpit. Ideally, each ACoA could find a spiritual director or pastoral counselor to help discern what are symptoms of their disease and what is truly love *as* Jesus loves. Many cannot, many will not, and many have not even recognized their own dysfunctional "love." Thus, for a preacher, who can reach an entire congregation, it is important not to reinforce unhealthy ways of loving but to search out examples, concrete and specific ways to "love as Jesus loves."

Some symptoms of co-dependency are lack of boundaries, addiction to one or more relationships, taking inappropriate responsibility for another, striving to be "nice," care-taking, turning the other cheek, a pollyanna "joy," giving second, third, fourth chances, fronting for another. These symptoms can look like unconditional love, and need to be discerned for the truth underlying them.

For example, sometimes a close union can pose as intimacy but is in truth an addiction to another. A sense of self may be so damaged, twisted or non-existent that one may take identity and meaning only from another. Fear of rejection and/or abandonment keeps the co-dependent "forgiving seven times seventy times a day," often without a word. He or she begins to build up a false self, a martyred self, the image of saint; the co-dependent takes pride in this virtue and may need to be "converted from goodness."[9]

Jesus was once afraid of abandonment, according to John's gospel (6:67). He turned to his closest friends, after some of his disciples refused to walk with him any more. He was not play-acting when he asked the Twelve: "Will you also go away?" If they too had turned aside, would not his sense of self, his identity as God's agent, have kept him faithful? He needed friends, but did not get his identity from them, was not addicted to them, would not sacrifice his integrity. He did not run after the rich man whom he looked on so tenderly (Mk 10:21), nor persuade and plead with his first disciples, but simply said "Come and see" or "Follow me."

"Since they have no boundaries, co-dependents take on another's sadness, happiness, fear . . ." writes Ann Wilson Schaef.[10] Others may applaud that fusion as compassion, but the co-dependent needs to look at Jesus' compassion to learn how he did not fuse with his friends, merge with his mother (Mk 3:21, 31) but grew in a clear sense of himself so that as a self he could offer a strong and steady self to others in misery. He did not make their decisions for them, act as caretaker, take responsibility for their actions or feelings. In promising them a counselor, the Paraclete, he did not, as co-dependents do, make himself indispensable; instead, "It is necessary that I go away . . ." (Jn 16:7).

"Turning the other cheek" and "loving enemies" especially can play into the dis-ease of co-dependents. Because they have such poor self-images, they become like "a bridge over troubled water" on which anyone can stomp. Co-dependents are noted for loyalty to a person, institution, cause, long after it is reasonably warranted. They can be addicted to banging their heads against a wall, thinking they are offering unconditional love. Turning the other cheek means becoming a punching bag, whether emotionally or physically.

Jesus, on the other hand, did not let people walk all over him. In his autonomy, he confronted not only the "enemies" of the burdened folk but his own enemies. He sized up loyalty to the synagogue and sacrificial system of his religion and broke with it. He acted as a law-breaker in his public life and was an outcast in his very public death. He would not give an inch to the Pharisees, Sadducees, Sanhedrin, Herod or Pilate. His silence during so much of his trial is interpreted by the evangelists to "fit" with Isaiah's image of a "sheep led to slaughter who opened not its mouth" (Is 53:7). He was anything but silent in his continual confrontations, as a layman, with the equivalents of Judaism's bishops. His silence before Pilate (only in the synoptics; in John's gospel he says plenty about truth and true authority) may be just as well interpreted as rage at the injustice being done him. He had the courage to say and do what he could, the serenity to accept the inevitable cost of his confrontations with organized religion, and the wisdom to know how to keep loving through it all: "Father, forgive them, for they know not what they are doing" (Lk 23:34).

Chapter 8

Teaching

Religious education of the young and the adult has experienced renewal in the past decades. Mainline denominations are asking religious educators themselves to continue their theological education and spiritual formation. Educators are thus better prepared to deal with the complexities which youngsters and adults bring to their search for God.

Teaching Children

Moving away from rote memorization of doctrine and Bible verses to exploration of children's experience and values encourages a child to a creativity and spontaneity so discouraged in a dysfunctional family. Fear of authority and its inconsistent use at home is reduced as educators offer consistent and firm boundaries. The need which children from alcoholic homes have for achievement and approval is redirected in a more exploratory, less mechanized or dictatorial style of teaching.

Teachers aware of possible chaos in the families of students may teach doctrine differently or emphasize new understandings. For example, in working with stories of Jesus' "miracles" with children it will be important not to present him or God as a deus ex machina, God-in-a-box, like a genie from a magic lantern. God does not do magic; Jesus is not sent to rescue but to be with. By teaching God/Jesus/Spirit as creators and animators of human freedom we can hopefully help children understand that God will not "fix" their families but will be with each member. God hates the abuse and neglect they suffer but God can only "kiss it"—not make it any better than a parent's kiss and hug can heal a skinned knee. God can listen to them, hug and reassure them that they are dear to God. We religious educators can reiterate that good news.

Do not feel, do not talk, do not trust are the unspoken rules which have governed generations of alcoholic families. Teachers of Bible class can emphasize stories which portray Jesus and other biblical characters as feeling strongly. Models like Moses, Hannah, Jeremiah or Mary who can (and do) say anything to God without fear can be offered as people who pray from their hearts. God's major actions, the exodus of Israel and the raising of Jesus, can be taught as the primary paradigms of God's desire for our freedom, a reason for trust and hope.

If religious education is to help children know God's love for them so that they might respond with a lifetime of learning to love well, then religious educators may represent a "normal" model of loving. The child's alcoholic parent is sick and the co-dependent parent's way of loving the sick parent often skews a child's perception of love. If the co-dependent model of "loving" is all a child knows, he or she may grow up to call subservience compassion, may call self-martyrdom self-sacrifice, may call enmeshed boundaries true loving union, may call lack of assertiveness or anger the virtue of patience.

Working with children in any form of ministry necessitates kindness, firmness and perspective. In the 1960s children were often polled about the qualities needed in teachers. Again and again, fairness and a sense of humor were ranked most important. With so many ACoA claiming their pain, now twenty to thirty years later, is it any wonder that these children then valued a consistent justice and a less burdensome perspective on living and loving?

Forming Youth

It may well be that those who minister to children and teenagers, whether in formal educational settings or the informal interaction of church scout groups, sports teams, dance or film or ski clubs, have more formation than information to offer the young. Doctrines never live so long in our hearts as do the women and men who influenced our hearts and minds when we were impressionable teenagers. "Formation" of the young has nothing to do with molding them into conformity and uniformity. It does have to do with being comfortable with their learning from our lives, not merely our lips. It presupposes our own Christian formation and continual transformation by the Spirit (2 Cor 3:17–18).

Educating Adults

Who has not participated in a Bible study with adults in which someone monopolized or someone had always to be "right," or someone obsequiously deferred to the ordained? If adult religious education counts on mutual sharing of faith rather than on imparting of doctrine, the sessions are open to all the various pathologies which ACoA may bring to groups, replicating their survival techniques during childhood years. Are there not the super-responsible, the humorous mascot, the withdrawn, the placator, the take-charge person in every gathering of Christians?

Ministers who lead adult religious education might experiment with methods which could prove healing for unrecovering ACoA. Faith-sharing might replace or at least be alternated with discussion. An androgogical method (as opposed to pedagogical, which assumes a child's *tabula rasa*) which focuses on each participant's experience in dialogue with a prepared lecture could draw out the quiet participants. Simplicity in scriptural interpretation might relax the super-achieving.

To exemplify the above methodologies . . .

Faith-Sharing

Since the building up of community is an outcome of effective adult religious education, a more community-oriented sharing could at times replace the minister's or theological expert's lecture. In a group of twenty, for example, invite each person to come prepared to share some lines from a favorite psalm, explaining the influence of that psalm on the person's daily living. Each might come prepared another time to share a favorite New Testament character, telling what the points of identification between that character and the student might be. There can be no rights or wrongs, no achievements or disgraces, since each is sharing faith, a relationship, an influence rather than a truth, let alone *the* truth.

Some adult education leaders assign a pericope or a chapter of scripture and open the session with small group sharing, even dyads, on just how the scripture spoke to the life of the student. Small groups and dyads relieve a lot of supposed pressure to perform. Again, no one can judge the student right or wrong, the interpretation as orthodoxy or heresy, since the assignment is to see how the scripture personally influences.

Because we are all (not just ACoA) so trained to get our religion "right" and to progress in the spiritual life, adult education sessions can often be the breeding ground of dissension, one-upmanship, and judgments of who is holier, deeper, more learned than another. Faith-sharing, however, can counteract that judging tendency, emphasizing as it does that each person's relationship with God (spirituality) is unique.

In faith-sharing, no comment is allowed to be made to the speaker. When absolutely no comment is allowed, not to the dyad partner nor to the small group sharer nor in a large group sharing (especially no comment by the leader), there is great discomfort at first. We are so used to needing/giving affirmation: "Oh, how beautiful an insight!" "What a profound thought!" etc. Unfortunately, even the most complimentary judgments usually include hidden comparisons such as: "such a profound thought" that I would never have; or "how beautiful an insight" which God never gives to me. We often judge our own spirituality most harshly, forgetting how uniquely God relates with each of us. No commenting keeps a co-dependent sharer from repeating the habit of external referencing and comparing.

After much practice of silent acceptance of another's faith-sharing, participants gradually lose their need to compare, and can then really listen, hear, appreciate what the speaker shares. This non-judgmental receiving, they report, is a mirror of how God listens so openly and acceptingly to our expressions of faith. Their receptivity one to the other is a foundation for building community.

Scripture Interpretation

Another kind of faith-sharing is modeled by the illiterate peasants and fisherfolk of Solentiname in Nicaragua. In the 1970s their priest gathered them each Sunday for a eucharist which opened with their explanation of the day's gospel. The priest would read a line of the gospel, and whoever felt moved would speak, uttering not an exegetical truth or doctrinal detail but a comment so homey, earthy, wise and reminiscent of Jesus' own.[1] Again, there can be no rights and wrongs, and judgment of each other yields to receptivity.

This method is obviously helpful in situations where adults are illiterate. The single reader is an effective tool too, however, with literate adults who need to check out every word. ACoA may betray their need for control by reading along, eyes glued to the text (sometimes in liturgical assembly as well). It would help their healing in trust to encourage them to listen rather than to read along, to look at the proclaimer with eyes and faces open to receive rather than physically to close themselves off, buried in a book.

Psalm 81 offers a bodily posture for prayer and listening to the word. God yearns: "Oh how I wish you would listen to me . . . how I wish you would open your mouths! I would feed you with the finest wheat and honey from the rock." The leader might start such an adult education session by asking students to sit with eyes closed, faces turned up, mouths open, hands spread upturned on their laps, like baby birds eager to be nourished by God's word, God's own self. After a moment of silent and bodily receptivity, the reader could begin the verse by verse reading/group comment.

Androgogy

Pedagogy is the method of teaching children; androgogy is the way to teach adults. In the United States, religious educators were among the pioneers in discovering how adults learn most effectively. Recently, Thomas Groome[2] and others have explicated methodologies which, in moving away from lecture per se, should help ACoA better trust their own experience and learning, take more responsibility for their lives and learning, integrate their intellectual searchings with applicable lived theology.

Sometimes adult learners are hungry for information, Groome admits. A minister or theological consultant may be invited to offer a lecture on a specific topic. One way to help the adults claim their own experience and God-given wisdom is for the presenter to ask the students first their own lived experience of the topic. Whether so esoteric a topic as the Trinity or so practical as women's ministry in the church, adults have experience and stories of their experience which will enrich the community and lecturer alike. If there is not enough time for the lecturer to hear all the stories in a large group, dyadic sharing or small groups allow the shy to participate more easily and confirm the lecturer/leader/minister's belief in them as having valuable experience and reflection on the topic.

Then the flexible lecturer can put the lecture in dialogue with the experience which the group has just shared, weaving some of their reflection into the prepared material. The lecturer then can return the responsibility for their own education to the adults, not by fostering questions to "the guru," but asking them to reflect on the material. The leader apportions some time for their silent reflection on what in the presentation affirmed their belief and what stretched their faith and/or practice.

Educating ACoA

Adult education classes in church settings usually treat scripture, doctrine, morality, spirituality. Recently, parishes and congregations have sponsored classes devoted to understanding the dynamics of growing up in an alcohol-centered family. Church basements are already the setting for many ACoA meetings. Educational sessions too are needed, especially to deal with religious issues such as guilt, shame, anger with God, images of God other than a parent-God, etc.

For example, a Lenten class (or perhaps two or three sessions) might deal with "Release from Guilt: Good News of the Cross for Adult Children of Alcoholics." First, the teacher might pray to the Spirit of truth to guide us away from denial and to reveal more truth, to help us remember what we need for our healing. Then the teacher would allow time for personal reflection on the topic. She or he might focus the reflection with a question such as: What has been your experience of growing up guilty? They may survey their young years, or perhaps dig more deeply into just one, but searing, incident. In a second session with a more theological orientation, "The Good News of the Cross," the teacher might take a more theological route: What has been your experience of the cross—good news or bad news? How did it come to mean that for you?

After three to five minutes for silent thought, the teacher asks the group to share in twos (dyads) or threes (triads). To enrich the sharing, if there is enough time, groups of five or six might be formed, but usually speaking to just one other in the opening of a session or series of sessions is less frightening. Later, larger groups might be used as the class begins to trust the open, trustful atmosphere which the teacher is creating, as the class becomes more accustomed to sharing in groups with others who understand and appreciate their experience.

Next the teacher would ask if anyone would like to share his or her own experience (not the partner's) with the larger group. A number who have experienced the release of feeling no longer alone, alien or judged may be eager to speak aloud, even in groups of fifty or one hundred. This gives the teacher, who has a lecture prepared, some experiential reference points, concrete cases to which the teacher may point as examples in the course of the lecture. The teacher is putting the lived experience of some of this particular group in dialogue with "the tradition," the lived but more universal experience as transmitted by researchers, thinkers, theologians on the topic of guilt and/or cross.

In the first session on guilt, unreal guilt might be examined, then stages in normal moral development explored, and finally participants asked to share—again after silent reflection—what true guilt, which leads to true contrition, might look like in practice.

Unreal guilt, the teacher might propose, stems from parental expectations. Even A's on a report card might not satisfy, for example. It may derive from expectations of oneself, a conflict between the idealized self and the real self. The real self, for example, a nine year old boy, wants to hoot and holler with his gang, but since his house must always be kept quiet because of mommy's headaches, he feels guilty when boisterousness breaks out, even on the playground.

The need to conform may be strongly ingrained in ACoA in order that those outside the family do not suspect the family secret. A conforming child can feel guilty about the most minor infractions of even unspoken family rules. One man shares a story of his boyhood on the farm where every creative or unique expression of himself with the land was labeled stupid by his farmer-father, just because it was not Dad's way. Guilt can even stem from the honest mistakes of childhood. In a trial-and-error experience of learning to live and grow, the child's errors are ridiculed, remembered, rehearsed before visitors.

Of course, teachers and schoolmates can reinforce unreal expectations, conformity, and make risk-taking look ridiculous. One of the major standard setters in a child's and family's life, however, is religion, the church authorities. While both parents and church can emphasize the debt a child owes to them *and* to God, thus fostering guilt, church authorities can set expectations of adult morality for little children. Sometimes those who hear the confessions of seven or eight year olds gently smile as the child tells of committing adultery. We can smile no longer. In such terror of mortal sin and hell, children who have twisted consciences from home can be further wounded by our church, and by ourselves, its ministers.

Some ACoA report they never feel they are good enough, worthy enough, have achieved enough spiritual maturity and so feel ashamed and guilty. Their guilt leads to deeper perfectionism and more desperate need to achieve salvation, to earn God's love and approval. Who can save them from this body of death, they cry, this circle of guilt which like a self-fulfilling prophecy may lead them to actual acts of sin, self-destruction and/or alienation? Only Christ Jesus! Christ is made tangible in the community of some of AA's offspring, for example, Overeaters Anonymous, Sex and Love Addicts Anonymous, Self-Mutilators Anonymous.

Because ACoA can only guess at what normal is, the teacher next points out features of normal moral development. For example, the following schema is based on the classic by Louis Monden, *Sin, Liberty, and Law*.[3] He demonstrates the progression from animal guilt and fear, through disappointment with oneself, to a genuine contrition in response to God's first loving us.

On the instinctual level which we share with animals, our morality is little more than a system of taboos. This "stage" is appropriate for little children, as Paul notes, who need the law as a tutor before growing into the freedom of which Christ is the source (Gal 4:1–11; 5:1). The law is external; life is ruled by shoulds, fears of breaking taboos and offending mysterious powers. Many adult Christians probably still view sin as transgression of law, whether God's, society's, church's or family's. They are, as St. Augustine put it, not afraid of sinning but afraid of hell. When they transgress, the urge to escape punishment drives them to external formulas and rites. Sometimes their confessions are compulsive, and in this extreme interior terror, called scrupulosity, they should probably be referred eventually by the minister to a mental health professional.

Monden's next stage of development is appropriate for the teenager and young adult. The focus is still on oneself, but law has shifted to the law within. This morality is dedicated to human growth, motivated by a desire for inner authenticity. If becoming fully human is the ideal, then sin is infidelity to self-realization. The sinner experiences a self-inflicted wound, and with honesty acknowledges the sin and firmly activates his or her will to change.

The final stage of morality is religious response, proper for adult Christians who have some experience of God and some consciousness of their relationship with God. There is no law to motivate them. They respond to God's initiative in their life. Not by their own striving, they come to a connaturality with God, a closeness which simply intuits what God wants moment by moment. Sin for them is a refusal to love, to respond. Their contrition is an appeal to the mercy of the beloved whose fidelity to them can transform their infidelity. Where sin abounded, grace more abounds (Rom 5:20) means that even sin is integrated into a deeper love and trust in God.

The teacher might at this point engage the students in some reflection and sharing on what true guilt and true contrition might look like in their own situations. When taboo times surface, as they always will since we regress from time to time, and ACoA perhaps more frequently than most in this area of guilt, it will be helpful to be more aware, to expose the "crooked thinking" in our taboos, and to thank God for this sign which reminds us of our lack of freedom and our need for God to save us from our guilt.

That is the good news of the cross. The cross, we may never forget, is an instrument of torture and injustice. The adults who participate in a session titled "Good News of the Cross" may have a lot of feelings to sort through and express about an abusive parent, God; about a Jesus who *could* have come down off the cross, could not he have?; about the stupidity of it all. It is important to share feelings in dyads or small groups and there will usually be anger, even rage rising up.

The minister has to be prepared for what may even sound like blasphemy, a cursing of God. No need for the teacher to defend God (ludicrous, is it not?) but simply to listen and receive the emotions: "Look what God did to Jesus!" After some large group griping, ask them to close their eyes and to breathe deeply, breathing out their fury, their feeling betrayed, their hostility, their fear and hatred of the cross, the bad news of the cross.

Is there any good news which flows from the cross? The teacher invites them to continue to breathe deeply, breathing in the Spirit of Jesus, asking the Spirit to teach them what might be good news. Let them breathe deeply for a while until the tension in the room calms. Gather what the Spirit has been saying to the church.

It may be opportune to teach new images of God, new understandings of God's will (see the previous chapter on preaching), new meanings of salvation. For example, salvation means being set out in the open, being given room to grow. It may be important to reemphasize Jesus' freedom, yet fear, in moving toward Jerusalem where he had to (inner authenticity) preach the good news of God's unconditional love (*his* response to God's love). Teachers may find from the adults' comments that the place to zero in is on the theme of life out of death or the Spirit's action of energizing what looks destroyed and dead (not only Jesus' body but parts of our lives too) into sources of new life.

After a final period of reflection on questions of what has affirmed their experience of God and what has challenged their experience of God, followed by some sharing, the teacher concludes with a question which reminds them that all education is for the purpose of action. What difference will this session make, do you think, in your healing, in your daily living and loving?

Of course, this prolonged example of adult education dealt directly with an ACoA issue and was addressed to those particular participants. Guilt or cross might be treated more generally. Healing is a topic, too, which many people want to explore, as best-selling books and overflowing retreat house programs testify. Whatever the topic, as poet Robert Frost asserted, real teachers teach themselves. Material and materials aside, an authentic, sensitive teacher who listens reverently to the thoughts, feelings, and most especially the experience of adult learners can be a catalyst for their healing and integrating their own personal history of salvation.

PART IV

The Ministry—
Helping Relationships

In our previous focus on public ministry, we noted a variety of ways for the minister to initiate the awareness, especially through preaching and teaching, that ACoA need healing. Now we offer a more detailed discussion of possibilities for long-term healing, especially through the therapeutic relationships operative in pastoral counseling and/or spiritual direction, whether one-on-one or in a group.

The most important human element in building not just a therapeutic relationship but any helping relationship is listening. First, then, we briefly review principles for active listening. Ministers are often sought out in times of crisis such as marriage preparation or separation, sickness, job loss, or death. After a few listening sessions, ministers may make referrals to specialized mental health professionals. We will treat crisis intervention and the process of referral as two short-term opportunities for ministers to offer help.

Pastoral counseling and spiritual direction may be two ministries for which the parish pastor is trained. However, pastoral counseling has long been professionalized in the Protestant tradition and more recently has been attracting Catholics with that special gift. Spiritual direction training programs have been operating within the Catholic community since the late 1960s, but now many Protestants are recognizing and fostering their gift for this non-directive ministry. The busy parish minister may want, and actually may be acting more responsibly, to refer the adult child in need of long-term healing to a minister who specializes.

Finally, with an explosion of lay ministries flowing from the recognition of each Christian's baptismal vocation to ministry, we note other one-on-one service. Our last chapter, though brief, is one of the most important: the minister's prayer for the healing of the currently battered, the previously scarred, and the recovering adult children in his or her community.

Chapter 9

Listening

Anyone in ministry is first of all a listener. If not in a formal sense as a spiritual director, confessor or pastoral counselor, certainly in a broader sense, ministers listen as we try to attend to and discern the real needs of persons to and with whom we minister.

Listening is a Judaeo-Christian stance. There are multiple pressures in our frenetic western world against the active receptivity and focused awareness on the here and now which listening requires. Our "here and now" is a noisy world with kaleidoscopic, multi-media blitzes on our senses and on our subconscious. These can overstimulate us into a state of numbed awareness and foster a passive receptivity which is a refuge from active listening.

The God of the Old and New Testaments models listening and attentive contemplation—for example, "God saw that it was good"; "God hears the cries of the poor." The story of the Hebrew people is a story of those who learn to listen to how God reveals fidelity and love in their human experience. Over and over again the word is spoken for our listening. Listening—availability to the experience of God, self, others, the world—is the opposite of the scriptural sin of hardness of heart:

> If only you would listen today! Do not harden your hearts as at Meribah (Ps 95:7–8).

Over and over again the plea of the psalmists to God is a plea for listening:

> Yahweh, hear the plea of virtue, listen to my appeal (Ps 17:1).

> God, hear my prayer; listen to what I am saying (Ps 54:2).

Very often simply the experience of being listened to is healing.
Is there any spirituality which does not encourage listening?

Listening to our own experience of God is reflected in nature, scripture, ourselves and others, the whole range of our human experience.

Despite how basic a listening, contemplative stance is, it is amazing how easy it is not to listen. We are tempted to be with others in a way which does not allow them to feel listened to.

Think about your own ordinary listening style, especially in ministry. Does it include any of the following obstacles:

- too much interruption.
- inappropriate self-disclosure: "Your story reminds me of the time I . . ."
- advice-giving: "What you need to do . . ."
- control of the conversation: "Let me tell you about . . ."
- passivity: failure to respond in ways which enable the other person to feel heard.

Listening Skills

There are numerous excellent texts in the various helping professions which describe the art of active listening.[1] A sampling of these are listed in the bibliography. Basically, listening has several components which can be described under the rubric of awareness, attending, and responding.

Awareness

First of all we need to become aware of our own listening style in general.

- Where is your own pattern on a scale between "talky" and "silent"?
- What in your body language facilitates your listening? What may block it?
- How accurately can you tune into your own "here and now"? What is going on in your life which may color how you hear another? (Fatigue, worry, any psychological or spiritual unease?)

Attending

The most basic component of listening is a cluster of attending behaviors, verbal and non-verbal.[2] The non-verbal cluster includes establishing and maintaining contact, especially through the powerful medium of the eyes. Eye contact is a way of directly engaging another. Sometimes its intimacy is too intense for some persons who may feel engulfed by this, but for most it is a gentle, direct way of respectful attending.

How and where we sit as we listen to others is another way of attending. Again, people have different requirements around comfortable distance and space. Ordinarily two chairs at a comfortable conversational angle enhance the atmosphere of attending. A desk can be a barrier to communication.

Posture is important. An attentive listening stance sometimes means leaning forward in a relaxed way. A relaxed posture is important because muscle tension can divert our attention from the person to whom we are listening. If you are someone who uses gestures, feel free to be yourself. Sometimes reaching out to touch someone in his or her pain is a gentle way of attending, although touch is a powerful medium and we need to be aware of its power.

There are certain verbal responses which are part of attending. Viewing a video of one of the masters, Carl Rogers, can be surprising as we watch the simple nurturing response of a "Yes." "Tell me more" and "I understand what you must be feeling" are other simple ways to lend attention and support to a person telling his or her story. Such simple verbalizations encourage and reinforce the person just as interrupting a story or selective inattention can discourage story telling. Experienced counselors learn to be sensitive to when persons might be using talk and story telling to distance themselves from connecting and exploring their own pain. It is best, however, to err on the side of listening rather than challenging, especially in the early stages of building a helping relationship.

Responding

What are some of the responses which allow a person to feel as though he or she has been heard? Accurate paraphrase is one way. Basically, paraphrasing is saying back to the speaker, in fewer words, what you, the listener, have heard. Ordinarily the person will confirm or correct your hearing. For example, an ACoA speaks:

> "My mother starts drinking about four in the afternoon and then I never know what to expect. One day she's mean and another day she's mushy. Sometimes I need to fix the whole meal and other days if I step in the kitchen she screeches at me."

Minister: "Your mother's inconsistency must confuse and upset you."

ACoA: "Yeah. I never know what to expect."

Sometimes as we listen, the story we hear is so vague and rambling that we are not sure what it is that we are hearing. In this instance, rather than faking understanding, it is better to share our confusion:

"I'm not sure what I'm hearing you say. Let me try to paraphrase what it is I think you're saying . . ."

It is important to check out the accuracy of our perception of what we are hearing. In the ordinary channels of social chit-chat we hardly ever do that. We seldom bother to check out innuendo or humor or how our own response to a person is heard.

Active listening also involves the invitation for persons to tell us more of their story and relate it at a deeper level. There are ways of leading a person to say some more. Simple responses like "How so?" invite the sharing of more of the story. Questioning can also be used, but it is important that our probing responses do not become too interrogatory. Sometimes a listener tries to manage his or her anxiety by gathering more and more data. The listener unwittingly, then, imposes his or her own illusion of control on the person's story by marshaling more and more facts. This can derail a person, however, from feeling heard and understood.

Reflecting is a level of responding which goes beyond paraphrasing. Too often we assume that if we accurately paraphrase the content, this is sufficient. We need to reflect, a skill which takes practice and experience to refine, on three levels. The levels include content, feelings, and process (or what we are experiencing right now in the room). These three elements are not neatly separated in real practice. Sometimes the content and feeling will be apparent and congruent or sometimes they do not fit together at all.

"I wonder what it means when you are sharing such a painful story with me but have a smile on your face."

Sometimes, something happens in the room which needs to be reflected. A person who is telling his or her story suddenly becomes distant or maybe starts tapping his or her foot or breaks eye contact.

Perhaps he or she is getting too close to his or her pain or is feeling threatened. The here and now process needs to be attended to and the person encouraged to go on if able.

> "I wonder what just happened. I'm picking up some anxiety in you and wondering what's going on."

> "I wonder if your foot could talk what it might say right now."

> "I'm curious about why you need to look away right now."

Sometimes these process reflections are too soon or too close and a person will resist them. The process takes time. Whether or not the person is able to respond at this point, at least the reflection allows him or her to feel heard.

It is impossible to overstate the healing capacity of active listening in ordinary ministry. There are many techniques available for uncovering and probing psychological wounds in a more clinical setting. They will not be discussed in any detail in this book because their effective practice requires careful training and supervision.

Chapter 10

Crisis Intervention

The purpose of this chapter is to acquaint the person in ministry with some of the theory and techniques used in crisis intervention. It is fairly well documented that one of the first persons to whom someone in crisis turns is a person in ministry.[1] Because a person in crisis can appear so disabled, it is helpful to understand some of the theory underlying crisis behavior in order to assess whether a person is suffering from a temporarily disabling crisis or dealing with a deeper, longer lasting kind of distress. Assessment is critical in determining whether to work with a person or to make a referral.

This chapter will also focus on how alcoholism can create a family situation where crisis becomes the norm. The adult child is frequently very adept at certain aspects of crisis management, particularly those involving the material or physical elements of survival. Sometimes it is a painful paradox for the adult child that the absence of crisis feels either dead or abnormal. Relative normalcy for ACoA can generate a state of disequilibrium.

Finally, this chapter will also describe a highly specified kind of intervention in which a person in ministry is often invited to participate: the carefully planned and structured intervention done with the alcoholic member of the family. Some adult children may have already had either healing or painful experiences with this kind of an intervention, so it is helpful for the minister to understand how it works.

Crisis Intervention Theory

Crisis has been part of the human experience since the beginning of time. The word "crisis" comes from a Greek word meaning "decision" or "turning point." The ancient Chinese character for the word means both "danger" and "opportunity." Both these ancient words capture the paradoxical nature of crisis in the human experience. It can be not only a time of extreme stress and pain but also an opportunity for growth and liberation.

While both the concept and the human experience of crisis have been with us for a long time, it is only during the past forty-five years that mental health practitioners have theorized and written about the experience. It is not surprising that what sparked the earliest study and writing was the human experience of grief. In 1946 Dr. Erich Lindemann published a foundational monograph, "Symptomatology and Management of Acute Grief."[2] Dr. Lindemann had followed the survivors of families who lost one or more members in the tragic Coconut Grove night club fire in Boston in 1942. He observed first hand the extreme upset and disorganization of acute grief and worked with persons as they worked through the crisis of bereavement. This was the beginning of what has become an avalanche of writing on death and dying and how persons cope with the stress of bereavement.

Dr. Lindemann became a colleague of Gerald Caplan, M.D., who wrote one of the earliest works on the role of community mental health policies and programs in preventive mental health.[3] Caplan hypothesized that a state of crisis is precipitated in an individual when their ordinary un-self-conscious equilibrium, internally or in relationships, becomes disturbed or disrupted. To the extent that there is an imbalance between the severity of the stressor and the capability of the person's internal and external resources to deal with the problem, the person experiences crisis. Habitual responses and behaviors work less well than they normally do. Often a crisis disrupts or removes significant relationships. Clearly, this is the continuing crisis which the adult child grew up with when one or both parents were not there emotionally and psychologically, if not physically.

The "crisis" inside of every crisis is that familiar coping skills do not work as well as they ordinarily work. Consequently, in working with a person in crisis the minister needs to help him or her either discover new coping skills or reframe the problem which he or she is facing and discover acceptable solutions.

Types of Crises

Theoretically, crises can be categorized either as *developmental*, that is, occurring in the normal course of human development, or *situational*. Developmental psychology identifies fairly distinct phases of human development which mark our journey from birth to death and some of the psycho-social tasks associated with each. Some of these markers are predictably stressful, for example, leaving home, marriage, parenthood, "empty nest" syndrome. All developmental crises call for adjusted coping skills and new ways of thinking and behaving.

Situational crises are more frequently labeled as "crisis." These include any of those hazardous events which profoundly disrupt life: sickness, death, war, accident, burglary, rape, tornado or any natural disaster, job loss, moving and relocation. In an old but still valid article, Reuben Hill (1958) presented a schema of how external and internal stresses affect family equilibrium.[4] He theorized that stressors which come from outside the family, for example, natural disaster, war, can solidify a family's capacity to deal with crisis. But internal stressors, such as alcoholism, suicide, infidelity, abuse, are experienced in a way which disintegrates and pulls families apart.

Differential Response to Crisis

Prior Life Experience

In your own work you may become curious about why one person is apparently able to deal with crisis and another person falls apart in the same situation. As you work with an individual or family it is critical to specify what exactly is the precipitating event or stressor. Sometimes a person's vulnerability to a particular stressor is shaped by his or her prior experience. A person whose early experience has included parental and other significant deaths may be more sensitive to loss as an adult. And while it is statistically true that the adult child is apt to marry an alcoholic spouse, it is also true that alcoholic behavior recurring in a later experience of work or love can be felt as particularly toxic and stressful.

Perception of the Crisis

Besides prior experience predetermining a person's vulnerability to stress, another major determinant is how a person perceives an event. Cognitive psychologists have served us well in demonstrating how cognition can impact emotion. And certainly the subjective experience of a crisis is going to be different depending upon whether the person perceives the stressor as a loss, a threat, or a challenge.[5] Loss usually makes a person feel sad and empty. Threat evokes anger or anxiety. Challenge evokes the more upbeat kind of anxiety which catalyzes rather than paralyzes. One of the strategies in working with persons in crisis is to help them reframe how they think about the stressor so that it becomes less overwhelming.

Characteristics of a Person in Crisis

When a person is in a state of acute crisis the feelings of upset and disorganization are profound. A person can feel as though he or she is going crazy because the emotions are so overwhelming. This extreme upset is often what the person in ministry sees and hears. Very often the person in crisis experiences not only acute emotional distress but also a variety of physiological upsets—sleep disturbance, gastro-intestinal problems, headaches, weakness. But since crisis is time-limited by nature, these acute symptoms do not ordinarily persist. If they do, it is a clear signal that the person is dealing with some more fundamental conflict or vulnerability than just the precipitating crisis.

ACoA and Crisis

Crisis resolution involves reworking of coping strategies. The tasks of crisis resolution can be conceptualized as *material-arrangemental* and *psycho-social*.[6] Adult children are often extremely adept with the first category of material-arrangemental but have more trouble with the second. For example, when there is a death in the family, no matter how acute the pain, there are definite arrangements that demand attention, such as funeral and burial arrangements. If fire or flood destroys the family home, shelter needs to be arranged. Too often the adult child, especially the hero, has learned from early on how to accommodate the material arrangements required by crisis. Being required to behave like little "homemakers" and/or "fire-fighters" they can cope with the material-arrangemental tasks which crises thrust upon them.

It is, however, the broader and deeper areas of the psycho-social tasks with which the adult child is less adept. This sometimes shows up as the adult child negotiates some of the normal developmental tasks. The following chapter on pastoral counseling highlights some of the struggles they face in relationship and intimacy.

Crisis, no matter what its particular outlines, can easily threaten a person's sense of security or competence or self-esteem. The crisis of death or divorce demands the adjustment to a new role at the same time a person is struggling with whatever feelings of loss, yearning, or unresolved anger may exist. The financial losses of being laid off a job or moving to an area where the cost of living is higher, or the physical losses precipitated by illness or accident, not only force a person to manage with reduced resources but also to cope with the frustration and anxiety of working out new solutions. The adult child who is cut off from his or her feelings and reluctant to trust whatever support network exists has a particularly difficult task.

Bereavement is a crisis in which the adult child may be particularly vulnerable. Death and bereavement are ordinarily among life's most stressful events. Grieving and doing the work of bereavement are more complicated processes for a person whose relationship with the dead person is conflicted. Even when some of the conflict has been dealt with prior to death, grieving becomes harder than the hard work it already is. When the alcoholic or abusing parent dies, it can provoke emotional disorganization inside the adult child which is more severe and long lasting than normal grief. The chapter on pastoral counseling discusses how mourning one's lost childhood is a major task for adult children. A major "moment" in this mourning happens when the parent dies.

Stimuli as Crisis Precipitants

Because the adult child grew up in a dysfunctional family and has frequently learned to deny and repress the pain of that situation, if an event or any stimulus breaks through the denial and repression, a crisis can occur. Emily Marlin reports the story of the young woman who became hysterical when her husband presented her with a plaid bathrobe for Christmas. The robe evoked an avalanche of painful memories of her alcoholic mother who practically lived in an old plaid bathrobe.[7]

Sexual Abuse

A particularly painful memory that can create profound crisis when it breaks through is the memory of sexual abuse which has been denied or repressed. If a person has been sexually abused, either a reexposure to the trauma itself or exposure/reexposure to events or stimuli which symbolize the trauma can precipitate crisis. When the trauma of sexual abuse unleashes intrusive symptoms in survivors it is deeply upsetting, especially if the person has had no conscious memory of being abused. Acute anxiety or depression, even severe decompensation (becoming temporarily psychotic), can occur and immediate crisis intervention by a professional is called for.

For the incest survivor even the "happy" developmental crises such as marriage, pregnancy, and birth can occasion the breakthrough of repressed memories. Or the death of the person who perpetrated the abuse can create enough of a safety zone for the person that he or she can begin to deal with the impact of the abuse.

Incest has long been a secrecy-shrouded taboo held in even more silence in families than alcohol abuse. The agonizing reality, however, is that possibly as many as twenty percent of the female population has had an incestuous experience at some time in their lives. As the topic becomes less shrouded in the silence of taboo, study and research accumulate which suggest its wider prevalence than previously believed. Today's media also tends to focus more on the topic, sometimes in unfortunately either a trivialized or a sensationalized fashion. Exposure to this kind of coverage can sometimes occasion the breakthrough of overwhelming flashback memories for the survivor. Memories and flooding anxiety can accompany these stimuli, as well as feelings of overwhelming rage at stories which highlight the fragility and vulnerability of abused children. This breakthrough of overwhelming feeling is often profoundly disorienting for the adult child.

Christine Courtois (1988) has written a comprehensive book, *Healing the Incest Wound,* in which she not only gathers and reviews the voluminous literature on the subject but also presents careful and thorough strategies for assessment, intervention and healing.[8] While it is primarily a book for trained mental health practitioners, it is also an extremely useful and highly readable work for anyone who wants to learn more about this profoundly painful trauma too often associated with alcoholically dysfunctional families.

Crisis Intervention Skills

There are two factors which distinguish crisis intervention from some of the longer term therapies. Crisis intervention is itself relatively short term and ordinarily it can be related to an identifiable stressor event or stimulus.

The first thing required in any kind of crisis intervention is to establish some sense of relationship and connection with the person in crisis. Very often, because of normal contacts within the ministry setting, that relationship already exists, at least embryonically. It is important to listen to the person's story of pain and how this event is impacting his or her life right now.

Crisis intervention calls for pastoral skills of reassurance and comfort. Reassurance consists of both a receiving and reverencing the pain of the other, and also an appeal to the strengths of the individual, assisting them to discover their own coping skills and strategies in dealing with their pain. It is quite different from a pollyanna reassurance which, in an attempt to cheer a person, can leave him or her feeling quite alienated and misunderstood.

During the phase of establishing a sense of connection with the person in crisis you need to be listening and simultaneously assessing whether something deeper is going on. What is bringing the person to you right now? Is there some identifiable stressor such as bereavement, job loss, some kind of family tragedy? You may think that you know the answer, but it is essential to listen to the person's own story of what is going on. Not only does this allow the person to tell his or her story and to let out some feelings, but it also gives you a chance to see how the individual perceives the event. As you reflect back to the person both understanding and feelings about the situation, together with a reasonable confidence in his or her coping ability, the person can begin to get a handle on the situation.

Part of the skill of crisis intervention includes an assessment not only of the individual's coping ability, but also of the support network and resources available for the person. Adult children are survivors of family situations in which the ordinary networks of family support may be underdeveloped, perhaps non-existent. It is helpful to discover what the person's support network is, wherever that exists.

It is also necessary to assess how the individual thinks about this crisis in terms of his or her self-esteem. If the adult child remains caught in the morass of shame and blame where what goes wrong is experienced as "my fault," the pastoral minister needs to be sensitive to this. It is not unusual under stress to regress to old ways of thinking and feeling, so it would not be unusual for the adult child, even if he or she is in a recovery program, to fall back into some old patterns of feeling excessively responsible or to experience self-blame and negative feeling about himself or herself. Such regression is normal, not to be argued about, but just accepted by the minister.

To accompany the adult child in walking through crises requires not only a repertoire of good basic helping skills, that is, attending, listening, and responding, but also referring skills. It is helpful to be familiar with the available community resources before you are faced with crisis management. Introducing yourself and making some personal connections with a referral network of community mental health providers is a good preparation for crisis management. If referral appears desirable it needs to be handled sensitively. Some persons have strong negative feelings about this. Some work may need to be done so that the individual does not experience referral as either rejection or abandonment.

Crisis events remind us of our creaturely limits and vulnerability. They can also remind us that life is not fair. The mother of eight has an aneurysm and dies two days before Thanksgiving. A father molests his daughter to "teach" her about sex. Christmas repeats itself as an annual ugly event because one or both parents are "celebrating" too much. Ministers at times of crisis often hear "Why did God let this happen?" or "Why did God do this to me?" This chapter is not the forum for a discussion of theologies of divine providence and will. But since in times of crisis the question often gets raised explicitly, it is helpful for the person in ministry to have prayed through and thought through his or her own personal beliefs. Jesus as the best image of God demonstrates a God who passionately desires to be with the poor, afflicted, and anguished in a comforting and compassionate way. But the God-who-is-with does not rescue us from the various profound human experiences of suffering. For many adult children, the God of their childhood from whom they sought rescue and relief has already disappointed them. Various crisis experiences can evoke this earlier experience. If a person's reaction to crisis is anger with God, it is important that the person in ministry can facilitate and bear the expression of that anger. To allow and to receive a person's railing at God can be a very healing experience for the person in crisis.

Intervention in an Alcoholic Family

This last section will focus on a very specific type of crisis intervention. Very often the adult child, particularly as he or she becomes more aware of the dynamics of an alcoholic family, wants to intervene with the alcoholic parent(s) in a way which will make it difficult for the parent to continue denying his or her need for help with alcohol. Old notions about alcoholics needing to "hit bottom" have been replaced by the reality that the family and significant others can "raise the floor"—that is, carefully precipitate the crisis (turning point) for the alcoholic. This strategy is named "intervention." Very often a person in pastoral ministry is invited to be a part of this intervention process if he or she knows the family. The purpose of an intervention is simply to convince the alcoholic person that he or she needs help in order to get sober and needs to enter into some kind of recovery program in order to do this.

Because denial is the family defense in an alcoholic family, very often the person who initiates the intervention will be dealing not only with the denial of the alcoholic family member but also with varying levels of denial among family members.

For intervention to be successful there needs to be careful planning and, ordinarily, some rehearsal. The intervention should be planned and facilitated by someone skilled in the dynamics and process of alcoholism intervention. The National Council on Alcoholism can provide names of persons in your area who are skilled in this process.

One of the first things which is done in planning an intervention is deciding who will participate. Often in addition to the family members, friends, colleagues, clergy, and the family physician are invited to participate. As persons in ministry your own understanding of the intervention process may give you the confidence to participate in the strategy if you are invited to do so.

The intervention specialist will explain the process in detail and demonstrate its usefulness in breaking through denial. Understanding the potential fatality of the disease of alcoholism, not to mention the relational and spiritual havoc of the disease, can help break down the denial of the family members and others who care about the person. The facilitator is responsible for taking a careful family and work history, and drawing out the impact of the person's disease on these. Careful and specific plans for the person's treatment alternatives are drawn up. If the treatment plan requires arrangements at a residential treatment center, this is done so that there can be an immediate move from the intervention to treatment if the person agrees to participate.

In preparing for an intervention the participants are asked to prepare very specific and concrete statements about how each observes the person's lack of control over his or her drinking behavior, the impact which the person's alcoholism has on each of the participants, and, finally, specific and concrete ultimatums which the individual faces if he or she refuses to participate in the recovery program.

While these statements can be simple, clear, and overtly unemotional, the process is laden with the emotional demands of "tough love." The process not only demands that the alcoholic enter treatment, but also requires the family members to make a commitment to their own recovery program and deal with their co-dependency and ACoA issues.

Because a lot rides on the intervention and because there are consequences for the alcoholic's non-compliance, the participants must be coached and need to be ready to follow through on whatever ultimatums are agreed upon, even when these can be quite painful, such as job loss until treatment is undertaken, and/or separation from family members.

Timing an intervention when a person is not expecting it and providing no loopholes for avoiding treatment is part of the process. Very often when the alcoholic is confronted by a number of persons in his or her life and is able to hear (even to a small degree) the impact of alcoholic behavior, the alcoholic's denial gets pierced. Because this breakthrough of the alcoholic defense is temporary, it is critical that all of the arrangements for transfer and entrance into treatment have been carefully orchestrated.

Despite its very careful planning and structures, process interventions do not always work. Sometimes the alcoholic's denial is too strong or anxiety so overwhelming that he or she bolts from the meeting. If this happens, the members of the intervention must stand firm on their ultimatum. A person in ministry who is part of this team needs to support this "tough love." Even a failed intervention is better than no intervention because it represents the family's attempts to do something about its own recovery.

Chapter 11

Pastoral Counseling

There are many excellent texts on the subject of pastoral counseling.[1] This chapter will not attempt to repeat or summarize them but instead will focus, for the person in ministry who is called to do pastoral counseling, some assessment guidelines and some of the focal issues involved in working through the "baggage" of growing up in a dysfunctional family. Pastoral counseling is itself a highly skilled mental health profession gaining increasing respect in the area of mental health care delivery. Its certified practitioners are rigorously trained and supervised and often work in pastoral counseling centers.

But it is not just to the intensively trained pastoral counselors that people in pain turn for the ministry of counseling.

The person in ministry is very often the person who gets to hear the story of a parishioner's pain. Just as the family physician or pediatrician often hears the tales of family dysfunction and suffering, the ministers of religious education or the pastoral associates often are chosen to hear a person's story if they appear to be good listeners. It is important for individuals who have not received formal training to be able to use their basic skills to listen well, begin to assess effectively, and know whether they can walk with the person or need to refer them to a more highly trained professional. In working with adult children it is also critical to know the self-help recovery groups which are available in the area.

Assessment

Listening is healing in itself and even sufficient in itself in various pastoral modalities. Counseling demands more.

Assessment is a listening stance which focuses on data gathering for the purpose of understanding what might be going on in a person or family to cause them pain. While assessment is descriptive in character, that is, a careful listening for issues, signs, processes, it also becomes prescriptive insofar as an accurate assessment gives a picture of some of what needs to be worked through in order for healing to take place.

There are many ways to approach assessment of ACoAs. There are self-tests for ACoAs, for example, which can be useful, especially if a person has some difficulty in owning family dysfunction.[2]

This chapter will review some of the basic issues which often are present for the adult child of a dysfunctional family. Each person's experience is unique and will present a different "shading" of the picture, but the issues outlined below are commonly experienced by children who have grown up in dysfunctional families.

Family Issues

The adult who grew up in a family in which alcohol was abused, depending upon the frequency and severity of the alcohol abuse, grew up in an environment which ranged from inconsistent and arbitrary at best to chaotic and abusive. The consistently "good enough" parenting which we need for nurturance and growth was not present in an alcoholic home. The alcoholic parent's drinking behavior could range from violently disruptive and intrusive to emotional and physical absence. The other parent, if not also substance abusing, usually suffered from the disease of co-dependency by which he or she tried to cover for the alcoholic spouse. In either case the children were emotionally deprived of their childhood. They lost that worry-free time when they could expect nurture, play, and relative freedom from adult burdens.

Roles

Family systems theorists remind us how critical the concept of balance is to any system. Families in which alcohol is abused develop their own balance in the rules and roles which are adopted for survival. Because in fact these rules and roles were literally necessary for survival, they are often held onto rigidly. Thus, as the children grow into adulthood, these rules and roles often interfere with healthy functioning in adult relationships. Claudia Black[3] outlines these roles:

The Responsible Child: This child (often the oldest or only) assumes caretaking responsibilities far beyond what a child should assume in the normal developmental course of learning how to be responsible. Often the house "manager," he or she becomes the one the other siblings learn to rely upon for cooking, household management, supervision. Sometimes this role achieves "hero" proportions and gets acted out in ways which society usually applauds, for example, outstanding academic or job performance. But the family banner-carrier seldom gets the chance to be a limited child or learn that perfectionism can be dangerous to one's emotional and physical health.

The Placating Child: This child is a manager of a different sort, the one who tries to keep emotions in the family balanced. This child puts enormous amounts of energy into making others feel better, even to the point of trying to rescue others from emotionally disturbing situations. Sometimes carrying the burden of feeling responsible for the parents' drinking, this child often grows up to marry a dysfunctional spouse.

The Adjusting Child: This child opts for peace at any price. Sometimes he or she becomes the "lost child," almost disappearing in the family in order to try to keep this rocky boat on an even keel. Lost children as adults report great amounts of time spent alone as children. They often grow up with the experience that the most manageable relationship is the avoided relationship. The lost child can grow into a loner.

The Acting Out Child: This has two manifestations. The less costly is the "mascot"—the little person who draws attention by entertaining. The other way of drawing attention—and fire—is to become the "scapegoat," the lightning rod child who protects the chaotic balance of the family by contributing to the chaos. Creating a crisis seems more manageable than passively waiting for one to happen. Negative attention is better than none at all. Very often this is the child who, if not helped, is most likely to become the next generation's alcoholic.

Part of an assessment strategy in listening to the story of an adult child is to discover which role (roles) he or she played in his or her family of origin. Since the roles are probably rigidly embedded because they were so necessary for survival, they are probably present and creating some tension (or unhealthy balance) in current love and work relationships. Since they also contain seeds of life and strength it is important to discover them so that the individual can celebrate the strength which they have sown for his or her adult life.

Rules

Every family system operates out of its own set of family rules. Sometimes these rules are clear and articulated. Sometimes they are fuzzy and unspoken. Sometimes they are a part of an ethnic or multi-generational legacy. Like roles, rules function in a family to achieve and maintain a certain balance and stability. Like the roles in an alcoholic family, the rules are fairly rigid. Claudia Black articulates the three overriding rules: "Don't trust. Don't feel. Don't talk."

The experience of growing up in an alcoholic family teaches a child not to trust. Unable to count on a parent for basic needs getting met, whether these be physical or emotional, the little person learns that the world is not a safe place to be. Because the people in his or her world are not trustworthy, the young person learns suspicion and mistrust and how to be on guard. Too often in dysfunctional families there is abuse. When the experience of emotional abuse (shaming, humiliating, mocking, threatening, betraying)[4] is compounded by physical and/or sexual abuse, the child learns even more deeply not to trust. If the child has been physically or sexually abused, the most apparently benign stimulus, if it triggers the memory of that original trauma, can be terrifying.

"Don't feel." Whether spoken or unspoken, this rule becomes a way of coping with what could be an overwhelmingly painful situation. Adult children of dysfunctional families often report difficulty in recognizing and naming what they are feeling. Some report an emptiness or a numbed feeling state. It is critical for someone working with the adult child to recognize that both repression of feeling and denial have served a purpose. To break down a person's defenses too rapidly can be dangerous. The assessment phase of working with the adult child is not the time to help a person recognize all of his or her feelings. This comes gradually during the process of working in a recovery program and/or professional therapeutic relationship.

"Don't talk." This third general rule covers an array of dysfunctional communication patterns. Very often a parent's drinking problem is the family secret. Certainly, physical and sexual abuse are kept secret unless their signs are noticed by adults outside the home. Often it is not the child's abuse but the spouse's abuse that is the secret. One ACoA tells the sadly common story of being afraid to go to sleep at night for fear that her drunken father would beat her mother.

Listening to the story of communication in a family, it is useful to watch for patterns and alliances of communication as well as for the topics which were taboo or family secrets. Very often in an alcoholic family the generational boundaries are loose. For example, the non-drinking spouse will depend on a child to meet the emotional needs which are more appropriately filled by a spouse. "My mother used me as her best friend."

If a minister decides to learn more about using genograms, this can be a very rich assessment tool in looking at the family stories. In addition to giving a visual picture of family roles and some important historical data, it also can show the patterns of alcohol abuse over several generations and be helpful in identifying other family agendas that seemed to be passed from one generation to another, for example, a pattern of conflict between mother and oldest daughter.

Self-Esteem Issues

A common burden of ACoA is low self-esteem. Self-esteem grows out of nurturing interactions with parenting figures, especially during the critical early years of separation-individuation. If a little person is allowed to grow securely into a separate "good-enough" person with enough positive feedback, then probably self-esteem issues will not be a problem. However, in a dysfunctional family very often the parents either do not themselves have a strong enough sense of self or are too preoccupied with their own anxieties to allow their children to develop a strong sense of self. Instead of being viewed and treated as separate, individual persons, parents often treat the child not as "other" but as a "self-object."

In ego-psychology "self-object" is the term used to describe the relationship in which another functions primarily to serve the self-esteem needs of the other and is not considered or treated as a person with separate needs and wants. In dysfunctional families in which children are treated as self-objects, only their behaviors which bolster parental feelings of worth and self-esteem will be affirmed and reinforced. Children are discouraged from a whole array of exploratory behaviors which enhance and test their own sense of self. Mistakes are not allowed. Negative rules—"Don't be angry," "Children should be seen and not heard," "Be perfect," "Don't cry"—stifle a child. Often the little person too early assumes responsibility internally for his or her chaotic environment. The negative feelings about self can lead to pervasive feelings of shame and guilt and a profound sense of being no-good. The experience of not being loved "well enough" leads to a sense of self as basically unlovable.

Being treated as a parental self-object can cause the child in his or her hunger for affirmation and approval to learn to stifle certain behaviors and become more adept at others. For example, "little mother," "comedian" and so forth can be roles which lend some balance to the tenuous family stability. In the process of developing these roles, however, a person sometimes develops a real split in his or her own sense of self. The outer "public" self may be extraordinarily competent but there is an inner emptiness and pervasive self-hatred which grips the "private" self. It is often the emptiness and blackness of the "private" self which eventually brings an individual to treatment.

Related to but not identical with self-esteem issues are issues of self-care. Flowing out of negative feelings about self sometimes comes self-neglect. Over- or undereating, poor self-care habits, alcohol abuse or other drug misuse can be a function of growing up in a dysfunctional family.

Feeling Issues

Very often the initial feelings described by ACoA are numbness and lack of feeling. This is hardly surprising given the need of ACoA to develop early on the defenses of denial and repression. Denial is perhaps the most pervasive element in the family disease of alcoholism. Despite strides in trying to counteract society's denial around issues of alcoholism, there remains a way in which society continues to reinforce denial by holding on to stereotypes of the alcoholic as a falling-down-drunk. Although there is better education today about alcoholism as a disease, the capacity to deny remains high.

Mary, an ACoA who is alone in the family in naming her father's drinking problem, tells this story from when she was seven or eight years old. Her dad was not an abusive or loud drinker. He would just become more quiet and unavailable. No liquor was kept in the house, but she had discovered pint bottles of whiskey in his pocket. One day when the family was out driving they passed a billboard advertising Seagram's. She asked her mother, "What's whiskey?" Her mother replied, "Oh, that's just medicine, dear." A few days later Mary took her mother's lipstick and crayoned over surfaces in the bathroom in big letters "IHW" (I hate whiskey). No one ever noticed or asked what the bathroom graffiti meant. Mary was a real mouse of a child, so presumably this extremely unusual behavior was noted but it was never named.

Repression of feeling happens when the feeling threatens to overwhelm in pain (or fear, or anger). It often follows trauma. Clinically, to have grown up in the dysfunction of an alcoholic family is being recognized as "Post Traumatic Stress Disorder." This designation, first outlined by the American Psychiatric Association in their DSM-III,[5] came with the recognition of the cluster of symptoms displayed by many of the victims of the Vietnam War. They include:

A.   The existence of a recognizable stressor.
B.   Reexperiencing of the trauma as evidenced by at least one of the following:
    1.   recurrent and intrusive recollection of event.
    2.   recurrent dreams of the event.
    3.   sudden acting or feeling as if the traumatic event were reoccurring.
C.   Numbing of responsiveness to or reduced involvement with the external world beginning some time after the trauma as shown by at least one of the following:
    1.   markedly diminished interest in one or more significant activities.
    2.   feelings of detachment or estrangement from others.
    3.   constricted affect.
D.   At least two of the following:
    1.   hyperalertness or exaggerated startle response.
    2.   sleep disturbance.
    3.   guilt about surviving.
    4.   memory impairment or trouble concentrating.
    5.   avoidance of activities that arouse recollection of traumatic event.
    6.   intensification of symptoms by exposure to events that symbolize or resemble the traumatic event.

The numbness associated with the trauma of growing up in an alcoholic family, especially if there was abuse or a fair amount of chaos, is a commonly reported phenomenon.

Sometimes instead of numbness the adult child reports other kinds of feelings, usually painful. Shame and guilt are two frequently reported feelings. Charles Whitfield makes the following distinctions between shame and guilt: "Guilt is the uncomfortable or painful feeling that results from doing something that violates or breaks a personal standard or value. . . ." Guilt is about behavior, whereas "shame is the uncomfortable or painful feeling that we experience when we realize that a part of us is defective, bad, incomplete, rotten, phoney, inadequate or a failure."[6] Shame is not about *doing,* it is about *being.* Sometimes the adult child has received direct verbal messages which directly compound guilt: "You never do anything right," or shame: "You g— d— rotten kid." Or sometimes the message is conveyed more subtly. But the feelings of both guilt and shame can be so awful that the very naming of these feelings is initially a great breakthrough.

Fear and anger are other important feeling issues for the adult child. Sometimes it is the free-floating nameless fear of anxiety, that sense of foreboding of something awful which keeps a person's insides stretched and knotted. Sometimes it is a more specific fear. Because denial is such a cardinal defense, there is the fear of being discovered. "If you really knew me you would . . . reject me . . . abandon me . . . laugh at me." There can be a fear of confrontation and conflict, a fear of feeling and expression of anger.

Anger in a dysfunctional or alcoholic family is often experienced as out of control. Anger is a powerful internal signal which our bodies send us when we perceive either a threat or a frustration of needs. The physiological component of anger predisposes us for "flight or fight." For a child growing up in a dysfunctional family there is often no alternative for his or her anger other than "stuffing it," swallowing it. Gerri, an ACoA whose father would get verbally violent in his rage, shouting abuse when he was drinking, is today terrified of her own anger which she barely allows to surface. Being around an angry person, even if she herself is not the target of the anger, Gerri feels very anxious and wants to leave the room.

As feelings long repressed for an adult child begin to emerge, the person finds them frightening and overwhelming. This experience will be addressed more fully in the section on "Working Through."

Cognitive Issues

The inconsistency and unpredictability of an adult child's family makes it difficult to know what is normal. So it is not surprising that many ACoA have patterns of "crooked thinking," distorted cognitive patterns, which in turn contribute to negative feelings. Many report "all or nothing" thinking, the tendency to see things in black or white. Sometimes the alcoholic parent is perceived as "bad" and the co-dependent parent as "good," perhaps as totally bad, totally good.

Another prevailing distortion is "personalization." The adult child, often because he or she is told "It's your fault," takes on a sense of responsibility for the family dysfunction. "If only I were . . . better . . . smarter . . . prettier . . . more athletic . . . then maybe Mommy or Daddy wouldn't drink." The disease of co-dependence demands this cognitive distortion in order to maintain balance in the family system. And because it is often subtly rewarded by approval or by a "martyr's crown," it can be difficult to correct. It is closely tied in to perfectionism.

Another example of "crooked thinking" is a type of "catastrophizing," that is, expecting and worrying about the worst possible outcome. One ACoA recalls his childhood terror in listening to what his father's footsteps sounded like when he came in the door. A slam of the door and a certain uneven footfall signaled a night of uproar.

When things seem to be going along smoothly there is the uneasy sense of waiting for the other shoe to drop. Behaviorists tell us that the most certain way to reinforce behavior is by a variable and unpredictable rate of reinforcement. Thus the unpredictability of the alcoholic disruption functions effectively to reinforce the cognitive mode of catastrophizing, waiting for the worst. No wonder ACoA behavior tends to become so rigid and controlled; perhaps they can contain the disaster.

Because the adult child does not have a good grasp of what is normal, some are prone to a gullibility. This gullibility is a type of the cognitive distortion called "maximizing" (or its reverse "minimizing"). This keeps us from seeing things as they are.

Joan is frightened to say no or refuse anything to her children. She grew up in a family where she was basically neglected emotionally. Today as the mother of two pre-teenagers she is almost burned out by their excessive demands. Afraid to insist that the children assume even minimal household responsibilities and afraid to set limits on their escalating demand for things, for time, for special trips to the shopping mall . . . swimming pool . . . softball/soccer/basketball game, etc., she is chronically exhausted and comes to counseling with the poignant but familiar theme of the adult child—"But I really don't know what *normal* is."

The last cognitive distortion which is often demonstrated by ACoA is "emotional reasoning." The most devastating example of this is connected to the profound feelings of shame reported by some adult children. "If I feel so bad about myself I must *be* that bad person." The internal feeling state is given an objective validity of truth. While it is very true that feelings are real and need to be reverenced, the internal feeling state is not always the objective reality.

Relational Issues

Much has been written in this area. Janet Woititz in her book *Struggle for Intimacy*, for example, provides an excellent overview.[7]

A key issue in any relationship is trust. A child growing up in an alcoholic family has learned not to trust the alcoholic parent for consistency of behavior, for keeping promises, for remembering, and for making reconciliation for outrageous behavior. He or she has learned not to trust the non-alcoholic parent for protection even when that person has tried to be a "super-parent" in an effort to compensate for the alcoholic parent's behavior. Most devastatingly, too often the adult child has learned not to trust himself or herself and his or her experience.

This understandingly creates some real fears of vulnerability which is demanded for relationship building. Because early experiences of trust are poor, the adult child is often fearful of disclosing his or her private self for fear that the true self will be rejected, abandoned or ridiculed.

Not having had a realistic experience of what is normal, very often the adult child has unrealistic expectations about relationships and is frightened by the tensions in relationships which are normal. Sometimes, if the identification with the co-dependent parent is very strong, the person will experience difficulty in setting limits, will tend to overfunction in a relationship at the expense of self. What may be wrongly labelled as "selfish" behaviors may be healthy "self-ness" behaviors, appropriate ways of caring for the separate self.

There may be struggles in the areas of separateness and boundaries. Boundary issues may be as "simple" as misunderstandings about tidying up one another's space or as deep as a feeling of being merged with the other person. Problems with separateness may show up in an inappropriate sense of responsibility for the way another feels and/or an unrealistic need to live up to the expectations of another.

Lastly, control is another significant theme for the survivor of a dysfunctional family. Because of the chaos and inconsistency of the family of origin very often the locus of control for the child would be whatever he or she could create. A need to be in control all the time makes the mutuality of an intimate relationship at best difficult to achieve. At worst, manipulation of the partner eventually strangles the relationship.

Strengths

No section on assessment is complete without a focus on the strengths which an individual survivor possesses. If a person is suffering poor self-esteem it might not be possible for him or her to claim strengths at the beginning of a healing relationship. It is important for the minister to be aware of some of the strengths which emerge and are fostered through the process of surviving in a dysfunctional family.

The adult child, particularly the one who filled the "hero" role, is often very responsible. He or she is self-reliant and knows how to work hard for a goal, even if sometimes too hard.

Adult children often have excellent "radar" about other people. The perceptiveness and sensitivity which they needed to develop as children can serve them as intuitive adults. They are often very astute at reading non-verbal signals and cues, although they need to check out the accuracy of these and not rely totally on the non-verbal cues.

ACoA may be quite adept at crisis management. They have learned how to be good "firefighters." As children many of them learned early to respond to emergencies and think on their feet.

In some dysfunctional families the alcoholism of one or both parents was a catalyst for bonding the siblings together. Even when the parental drinking was not explicitly talked about, the children looked out for one another and learned ways of cooperation which serve them well as adults.

In summary, the above issues name some of the realities which the adult child must deal with. Listening for the presence of these experiences might alert the counselor to a person's history and pain of growing up in an alcoholic or dysfunctional family even before the person is able to name this clearly.

Working Through

If a person in ministry receives the pain of an adult child, his or her first responsibility is to ally with the individual in a mutual commitment to the individual's own recovery process. This can happen through several channels. The last decade has witnessed a proliferation of self-help groups based on the Twelve Step recovery program. Alcoholics Anonymous, the "granddaddy" of the Twelve Step programs, remains the most effective modality for maintaining sobriety. Al-Anon and Al-ateen, the groups originally designed to support spouses and children in learning healthy detachment from the alcoholics' drinking behaviors, addressed the issue of co-dependency before the concept itself was framed and written about. In 1983 the ACoA self-help movement officially got underway and has grown immensely. The 1980s have also witnessed numerous self-help recovery programs addressing other addictions, also based on the Twelve Step program. Knowing the available resources in the community where you serve is very helpful.

It is also helpful to develop a network of mental health providers to whom you are comfortable referring a person. Mental health delivery has its own professional pecking order. It is important, however, to recognize that competence and expertise in this field is a function of experience and ongoing professional development, and not necessarily a function of the letters behind the provider's name. Sometimes insurance companies will dictate the choice of providers of care, particularly if the person is enrolled in a health maintenance organization (HMO) or other kind of managed health care program. The critical issue in referring a person for individual or group therapy is whether or not the mental health professional is thoroughly grounded in an understanding of alcoholism and co-dependence as family disease processes and has an understanding of and respect for the Twelve Step recovery programs.

A distinction between pastoral counseling as a profession and pastoral counseling as a ministry is probably in order. While adamantly holding onto ministry as its keystone, the profession of pastoral counseling as it has been defined and regulated by the American Association of Pastoral Counselors and the academic programs certified to grant degrees in this field is a counseling discipline which integrates psychiatry and theology. Its practitioners who are certified by the AAPC have demonstrated clinical competency after logging the required hours of supervised clinical experience. The minister who is certified as a pastoral counselor has been rigorously trained in the counseling profession.

On the other hand, persons in ministry are frequently sought out for "pastoral counseling" because of their ministerial identity. Most contemporary seminaries do include basic requirements in helping relationships and a foundational course in pastoral counseling. These, however, do not prepare an individual to do any kind of long term counseling. Any counseling which moves beyond the supportive into areas of uncovering and reworking old defenses should be done only by someone trained in a clinical profession.

It is helpful, however, to become familiar with some of the recovery work which the adult child will be experiencing in counseling in order for the minister to support his or her journey to wholeness. The pastoral counselor working with the adult child, in addition to supporting his or her commitment to recovery, needs to understand some of the "here and now" issues which the adult child is working through.

Part of the healing comes in the telling of the story, the literally painful "re-membering." As the story is retold and some of the old feelings which were denied and cut-off are gradually re-membered and received by a supportive and empathic listener, healing starts to happen. The re-membering of the story, particularly if the trauma has been severe and deeply repressed, can be extremely painful, accompanied in some instances by sleep disturbances, nightmares, anxiety or depression. It is critical to let the individual loosen his or her own defense of repression at a pace which feels safe, especially as trust is gradually developed. Probing and uncovering needs should be left to the trained clinician.

Basically, the work of recovery can be conceptualized in a number of ways. They all incorporate the elements of mourning a lost childhood and discovering and enhancing the self which was never allowed to emerge, either as individual or in healthy relationship.

Mourning

Mourning or grief work is the normal, healthy way to resolve loss. Society long has recognized death as the ultimate loss. Religions have developed their own rituals to facilitate the mourning process. Loss is very much a part of being human, a painful limit imposed by the human condition. Loss can be timely. Each of the developmental crises carries an element of loss which contributes to the disorienting experience of loss.

What are some of the losses of the adult child? He or she has lost childhood in some real ways. Very often the experience of growing up in a dysfunctional family means loss of trust and love and in some cases even loss of provision for basic survival needs such as food, shelter and physical safety. Additionally, ACoA may have actually lost the parent in divorce or death.

Since denial has been the predominant family defense, most adult children have never been allowed or allowed themselves to grieve their unnamed losses. Unresolved grief almost always goes underground to reemerge later in life as chronic depression. Loss of energy, persistent fatigue, low self-esteem, feelings of shame and guilt, feelings of hopelessness and helplessness, anxiety, irritability, weepiness, sleep and appetite disturbances are some of the signals of chronic depression in addition to persistent feelings of sadness and inability to enjoy life. Some people who complain of inability to concentrate and to make even minor decisions are surprised to learn that this not particularly sad expression is yet another true expression of depression.

Sometimes this chronic depression is masked and defended against by compulsive activity and perfectionistic kinds of striving. Becoming "tireless" and "limitless" caretakers of others defends a person against his or her own neediness and yearning to be cared for. Sometimes physical illness represents a legitimate way to get needs met and the only acceptable way to set limits. When the "crash" comes after excessive caretaking and/or other kinds of achieving, it is often accompanied by depression.

In order to do the necessary grief work the adult child needs first of all to get in touch with his or her own inner child who has been neglected, squelched, abused and in some cases even tortured. Sometimes an ACoA can be directed to fantasy, sometimes to contemplate a child, sometimes to look at old photo albums to get back in touch with the little boy or girl he or she once was. Bill, a forty year old ACoA, has a picture of himself at nine years, wistful with his bat and glove. It helps him connect with and feel compassion for the little boy whose daddy was never available for baseball. Mary, a competent forty-five year old administrator, can finally begin to nurture her five year old who sits frightened and crouched away from the young, strained, alcoholically abusive mother staring from the porch into the camera.

A main "work" of childhood is play. Too often the adult child has not had the opportunity for much free play. His or her play was too often under the shadow of the unpredictable behavior of the parent. Marie recalls the pain of being ordered at the last minute to cancel her eighth grade sleep-over party because her alcoholic mother whimsically chose this opportunity to "character train" her child and teach her "obedience."

Sometimes it is helpful to invite the adult child to study a child at play. For example, watching little children at the beach gives a wonderful opportunity to learn how a child plays. Children are totally absorbed in building the sand castle. They shriek in delight, darting in and out of the surf. They take risks, let their little bodies be kissed by sea and surf and sand and sun, a totally sensate experience. These elements of child play—focused absorption, sensate appreciation, risk taking, unashamed delight and laughter—need to be relearned.

Too often the experiences with parental touch which adult children have had range from non-existent to negative so that they can be generally uncomfortable with the body or cringe from touch. They deny the nurture and comfort of touch and other sensate experiences. Learning to look, listen, smell, taste, touch need to be reaffirmed as the adult child, while mourning his or her lost childhood, also makes friends again with his or her inner child.

Too often the adult child was nurturer rather than nurtured as a child. Learning simple ways to nurture oneself and not feel guilty about this is part of the healing process. Something as simple as taking a long, luxurious bath or allowing oneself to take the phone off the hook or budgeting something extra just for fun are simple ways a person can learn self-nurture. These are opportunities in addition to the basic and necessary self-care of balancing good diet, rest, exercise and play.

When a person has been able to mourn a loss effectively, that is, move through the phases of numbness and the often disorienting experience of intense and ambivalent feelings, the yearning and seeking for the lost object, then the final phase is the letting go and moving on. For the adult child this means that eventually one is able to surrender to the reality that what happened chronologically in childhood cannot be changed. By reconnecting, however, with the inner child and getting a clearer sense of the emergent self the person is able to be clearer on what he or she is able to change. This *active* surrender eventually allows for the forgiveness of parents and family, although during the working-through process these might still be "toxic" people. If the adult child needs to avoid them for a while the minister ought to support this and help the individual contain self-blame. While forgiveness is an eventual goal and probably the final act of letting go, it is not something which can be forced prematurely. Even in a psychologically therapeutic setting, forgiveness of "those who trespass against us" is God's gift given in God's own time.

Too often adult children have been discouraged from developing as true and separate individuals. "Self-ness" behaviors have been labeled as selfish. Learning new skills and behaviors are part of this necessary working-through. Feelings which might have been labeled bad or unacceptable need to be reclaimed. Harriet G. Lerner's *The Dance of Anger*[8] is a helpful book in learning about anger and how this emotion is useful in becoming clearer about oneself. Although written primarily for women, it can be read profitably by anyone who has grown up in a dysfunctional family. The experience of anger is often a clear signal that one is allowing oneself to "de-self," that is, sacrifice or betray self for the purpose of maintaining peace in a relationship. This is *not* the mutuality demanded in any healthy relationship but the consistently one-sided sacrifice of self which sometimes happens to keep a balance in co-dependent relationships.

Expression of anger does not have to be a rehearsal for World War III. It can be a calm, clear expression of needs, expectations, negotiations. One of the skills which the adult child often needs to learn is assertiveness and conflict resolution. Unfortunately, in an alcoholic family, some children may survive by aggressiveness, manipulation or passive aggressive behaviors. A yearly outburst of anger by the long-suffering "martyr" co-dependent parent may threaten family security beyond belief simply because it is so "out of character." This is quite different from that assertiveness which claims one's dignity as a person and demands to be justly treated.

Very often the adult child needs to become aware of his or her own patterns of automatic negative thinking. *Feeling Good: The New Mood Therapy*[9] by David Burns, M.D., is an excellent self-help book in this area. Burns offers concrete exercises which are useful in correcting these patterns.

The adult child usually needs to learn new relational skills. Taking risks in self-disclosure and giving feedback need to be learned gradually and safely. The one-on-one relationship of counseling is a safe place to learn self-disclosure. However, group therapy or a support group is probably the most effective way for ACoA to learn the mutuality of the interpersonal skills necessary for developing intimacy in relationship.

Throughout this process of working through, the minister needs to understand that the adult child has to have "tonic" rather than "toxic" relationships. The support of recovery groups and hopefully the church community itself can be "tonic" rather than "toxic." A minister needs to be aware and sensitive, for example, that for the adult child events such as birthdays, holidays, anniversaries, weddings can be toxic instead of the joy-filled experiences which our childhood myths make of these events.

The process of working through the trauma of growing up in a dysfunctional family takes varying amounts of time. If the individual has shared his or her therapeutic process with the minister it is help-ful to be sensitive to the process of termination of counseling or therapy.

If termination is timely and not dictated by a limit imposed by insurance coverage, the individual will have had the chance to con-solidate new strengths and to let go of old hurts. He or she will have had the chance to work through attachments and/or negative feelings toward the counselor.

Leaving a good counselor, like leaving a good home, is bitter-sweet. The challenge and excitement of getting on with life is a stronger pull than staying in the comfortable "home" which a helpful counseling relationship becomes.

Sometimes the power of leaving the counseling relationship is underestimated. If termination happens in an untimely fashion it can complicate in a counter-therapeutic way the adult child's fear of abandonment. Any minister undertaking or supporting a counseling relationship needs great sensitivity to this issue.

Conclusion

As noted in the beginning of this chapter, pastoral counseling is both a ministry and a professional mental health discipline. In the specific area of working with adult children the minister offering either kind of service can amplify his or her own understanding by the numerous, highly readable books on the subject. As in any pro-fessional area, skills for working with and understanding of adult children can be sharpened and enhanced by taking advantage of professional development opportunities. Books, workshops, supervi-sion and professional networking are some of the ways that a person in ministry can further develop his or her counseling skills and expe-rience.

Chapter 12

Spiritual Leadership

At the heart of the ministry of spiritual leadership, spiritual direction, spiritual development, spiritual reflection is the Spirit, source of human spirituality. Spirituality is at the core of the conversion and continual transformation of the recovering alcoholic and other kinds of addicts, including the para-alcoholic, the ACoA.

The Twelve Step program of Alcoholics Anonymous and its numerous offshoots was born through a profound religious experience of its co-founder, "Bill." In November 1934, after many attempts at rehabilitation, even hospitalization, an old school friend arrived while Bill sat at his kitchen table, guzzling gin. This friend had been committed for alcoholic insanity but now, sober, he announced to Bill, "I've got religion." As they continued to talk, Bill shut his mind to the God of the churches, but his friend encouraged him to choose his own idea of God.

> That statement hit me hard. It melted the icy intellectual mountain in whose shadow I had lived and shivered many years. I stood in the sunlight at last.

> It was only a matter of being willing to believe in a Power greater than myself. Nothing more was required of me to make my beginning.

Once before, during World War I in an English cathedral, Bill had "needed and wanted God" and God came to him. Now after a final detoxification in a hospital, Bill was ready.

> There I humbly offered myself to God, as I then understood Him, to do with me as He would. I placed myself unreservedly under His care and direction. I admitted for the first time that of myself I was nothing; that without Him I was lost. I ruthlessly faced my sins and became willing to have

my new-found Friend take them away, root and branch. I
have not had a drink since.

As he sat quietly in subsequent days, Bill turned to the "Father
of Light" for direction, expecting to receive in great abundance.

. . . the effect was electric. There was a sense of victory,
followed by such a peace and serenity as I had never known.
There was utter confidence. I felt lifted up, as though the
great clean wind of a mountain top blew through and
through. God comes to most . . . gradually, but His impact
on me was sudden and profound.

Bill saw, too, the importance, the necessity, of ministering to other
alcoholics as an essential step in the healing process.[1]

Bill's friend "got religion" but Bill got spirituality, a belief and
trust and love of a personal God who Bill realized is at our service,
ministering to our spirit when we open to God's ministry. It is God's
ministry which we embody when we provide leadership and/or
companionship to those hungering and thirsting for God. We might
offer that companionship called spiritual direction, but first we will
examine some other types of pastoral care of the spiritual life.

Some Ministries Related to Spiritual Direction

As must be obvious from our chapter on pastoral counseling, it
may be that a person who inchoately knows that he or she needs
counseling will choose instead to ask a minister for some form of
spiritual direction. It is a less stigmatized form of pastoral care. It also
may seem less threatening to some seekers, both because God is
involved and because they believe they can divert the focus from
themselves. As we will see, the dynamics of an incarnational, scrip-
ture-oriented spiritual direction are somewhat similar to the dynamics of pastoral counseling. We will also ponder confession (which
in Roman Catholic communities may become a face-to-face celebration of the sacrament of reconciliation), guidance of individuals in
prayer and the structuring of faith-sharing groups. Only then will we
elucidate spiritual direction itself.

Confession

In the first Christian community there was no rite of reconciliation other than baptism. For the ordinary sins and failings of daily life, one confessed to another lay person, whether spouse, friend or the injured party. Even after the order of penitents was established as a chance for forgiveness of grave sin after baptism, lay confession continued—and continues to this day. Whether to the ordained in the rectory office, to the youth minister during a rap session, or to the sister who visits the nursing home, Christians continue to confess their sins and their sinfulness.

It seems a prudent rule of thumb to accept a person's confession of sin as the person presents it, without argument, or even question. In a one-time burst of sorrow, it is most important for the person to feel heard, understood, accepted and thus forgiven by one who represents Christ.

It may take a person, especially an ACoA, a number of sessions to express the pain within. Sometimes that confession will be made to a lay pastoral counselor or spiritual director as well as to an ordained minister. If the sessions are few and the pain, especially guilt and shame, is simply expressed, we probably are dealing with a "confession" rather than a search for long-term healing. Women ACoA will, for example, often look for a woman officially designated by the church with whom to share memories of sexual abuse. It is the shame and guilt confessed as well as the hunger for God's acceptance which makes this "confession." Just bringing the pain to light, to another human being, almost always provides relief and perhaps even some deep healing. After all, reconciliation is meant to rectify alienation and isolation.

In the Roman Catholic community, the rite of reconciliation has been renewed. The chance for face-to-face conversation with the one confessing offers the priest an opportunity to form or reform conscience and to probe with the person for the roots of sin.

The conscience of an ACoA is often twisted by non-existent or inconsistent morality of the parents. The disease of the alcoholic was undoubtedly labeled sin. Thus, the alcoholic who misses mass on Sunday, for example, is viewed as a bad person. This can trigger a terror in a child that he or she will be separated forever from the "sinful" parent. It also can lead to a taboo morality in which church rules forgotten, neglected, broken or defied take on a terror of their own, even for an adult. Often these rules center around impression management, the public sins such as missing mass, eating meat on Friday (once), drunkenness, angry outbursts, vulgar or curse words. Taboo morality, described in Louis Monden's *Sin, Liberty, and Law*,[2] while appropriate for little children can border on the pathological in adults.

It is a taboo morality which often leads to compulsions. Having something drummed into our impressionable minds can lead us to want those very things which are so vociferously forbidden. The things I do not want to do, I do, laments St. Paul (Rom 7:15, 19). A priest who as a regular confessor receives again and again the sad and shame-filled self-accusations of masturbation, gambling, overeating, lying, stealing little things from the office, or shoplifting substantial items needs to name these "sins" as compulsions and needs to help reform a childish conscience into an adult conscience.

Obviously, the issue is freedom. Taboos terrorize into slavish conformity. Our God desires our freedom from compulsion. The Twelve Step programs offer a way through compulsive and addictive behaviors: first, acknowledgement of the behavior and human helplessness; second, belief that God wants to and will save (save, not rescue; save is from the Hebrew *yeshua* meaning to set free in the open); third, a handing over the compulsion, guilt and shame to God, turning life, control, will power and the lack of it over to God. Then only does the addict make a moral inventory, a "searching and fearless moral inventory," and admits to God, self and another "the exact nature of our wrongs." The sixth step, complete readiness "to have *God* remove all these defects of character," does not count on human will power but on God's freeing action. "Humbly" asking God to remove these defects, the seventh step, is perhaps a key. The steps spring from the humiliation of hitting bottom, experiencing powerlessness, and lead to the humble begging for God's love, healing and salvation.

A confessor might consistently use scripture passages on humility or freedom to open the sacrament. He might create penances to break into small steps some concrete ways toward healing. For example, the penitent might be told to take a walk. That is "penance"? "Get into the midst of some beauty," the confessor continues, undaunted by the sinner's desire for humiliation and painful practice. "Breathe deeply, listen carefully, look all around at beauty and know that God looks on you so tenderly, God would give whole worlds of beauty (Is 43:4) for you."

Another area of "sin" which ACoA are likely to bring to confession are feelings. Then the confessor might prepare to open the rite by choosing psalms or passages from Jesus' life which demonstrate various emotions. Books such as *When You Are Angry With God*[3] or *May I Hate God?*[4] take some powerful, frightening, painful passions to their outer limit. God gave us emotions to signal and motivate action; they are God's gifts. We need not water down our anger as "justified" (like Jesus' cleansing the temple), or call God's jealousy good while ours is, of course, bad.

ACoA especially tend to equate feeling with behavior, thoughts with action. That is a Christian cognitive disorder, traceable in part, no doubt, to Jesus' saying that lusting in the heart *is* committing adultery. In context (Mt 5:27–28), Jesus was inviting us away from an externally referented, taboo morality, helping us to internalize our morality. It is not enough for adult Christians to keep outwardly the natural law against adultery. Our hearts are to be chaste.

Jesus' statement

> . . . does not mean we are not to admire a beautiful person or want to be sexually united with a good person but that we are not to use another, even in our private thoughts. We may be tempted to use another. We can, if we are not afflicted with a compulsive personality disorder, choose not to use someone, even mentally. Wants, thoughts, ambitions, even lusts, need not be denied, repressed, quickly buried. These movements of the human spirit are important to our own growing in wisdom and grace and help us to discover and discern what will please God.[5]

In forming or reforming an ACoA conscience, a helpful confessor leads gradually away from a taboo morality with law as the external referent. Some penitents, however, get stuck at the still youthful morality based on internalized standards. ACoA are connoisseurs of shame, disappointment with themselves for failure to meet not only the expectations of others but their own standards of perfection. Again, this may be another Christian cognitive disorder in which human beings refuse to be creatures, to be human, thinking themselves to be God: all-knowing, all-powerful, all-responsible, all-perfect. As we have seen, the God of scripture is not even so perfect as they would strive to be! This is the underlying wisdom beneath some AA slogans: Let go and let God; Easy does it; Let God be God.

All the while these adult children, tormented by shame, are "sorry" (repeating "sorry" to those whom they encounter throughout their day) their eyes are squarely fixed on themselves, their failure, their progress, their sin, their spiritual achievements. Pride, refusal to be creature, which is the recurring sin noted in the Jewish scriptures, undergirds their thinking and doing. Adam and Eve wanted to be like God, wanted to know for certain just what is good and what is evil. Then they could judge for themselves. God is the only one who knows; creatures might struggle to know, but ultimately must trust their goodness and their evil to God. Cain thought he was master of life and death; the builders of the tower of Babel thought to penetrate heaven. King David, who arranged to marry Bathsheba by sending her warrior husband to his death at the front, was faulted by God for taking matters into his own hands.

Is there a remedy for this kind of refusal-to-be-creature pride? "Let us run the race in which we are entered, eyes fixed on Jesus" (Heb 12:1–2). Eyes fixed on Jesus, not on self, working so hard to impress God. Monden's most adult stage of moral development presupposes that adults know God/Jesus/Spirit personally, are alert to the blessings poured out throughout their day, can find God even in distressful times, and are free enough to respond to God's initiative. How to develop or deepen a response-morality? Eyes fixed on Jesus, whom we can meet in prayer.

Guidance in Prayer

Christians who take their spiritual life seriously (and adult children often swing, in their extremism, to the very committed side of the spectrum) may approach a minister to learn how to pray or to pray "better." This is more a call to teach than to facilitate a life of prayer, but it is a welcome sign of a congregation's vitality. While the minister may teach various forms and techniques, some ways to pray may be especially helpful to ACoA.

First, it would be important to understand why this person wants this instruction and why now? How does this person define prayer and describe his or her contact with God up to this point? Who is the God to whom prayer is addressed? Questions such as these may provide openings for a minister to deal with some ACoA issues without ever needing to ask bluntly about the person's family of origin.

Obviously the chief issue centers on God. Who is God, how does God operate, what does God "do" with our prayer? God cannot be manipulated by prayer, not even by fasting. God, in total freedom, takes the initiative in every human relationship with the divine. God has given the desire to pray, God has given the Spirit who prays within us. It is especially helpful for adult children who so often need to control prayer and produce at prayer to ponder the good news that when we do not know how to pray as we want, the Spirit puts our most inarticulate groanings deep within into language which God can understand (Rom 8:26). Praying, uniting us with God, is the Spirit's work (Rom 8:15), not anything we need to achieve.

Bodily Prayer

Because ACoA can hide many inarticulate groanings even from themselves, it is helpful for them to learn to be quiet inside before they turn their attention to God within. They might center themselves in the God who is living, breathing, loving deep within them by breathing deeply. If they cannot quiet their minds and hearts at once, they might try breathing out the worries of the day on one deep exhalation, the hurts of the day on the next, then the resentments, sorrows and so forth. Then, on each inhalation, they can image themselves within God, breathing in God's peace, breathing in God's joy, God's gentleness, God's kindness and so on.

They might breathe in tune with the Spirit who is known in scripture as the breath of God. The Spirit cries God's name from deep within them, linking them to God. St. Paul writes that the Spirit cries "Abba," Daddy (Rom 8:15). If that is too painful an image of God, and "Mommy" does not fit either, they can insert their own name for God or ask the Spirit to reveal God's name. Repetition of that name while breathing deeply leads to two healings: first, the ACoA is not "working" at prayer which is as simple as "breathing out and breathing in" (a line, appropriately, from the song "I've Grown Accustomed to Your Face" which is what prayer is about); second, the ACoA has direct experience of God's initiative, the Spirit's work of prayer.

Today many Christians are fascinated with eastern meditation. They strive to blank their minds and empty themselves of desire. This has some merit, especially when taught by Christians steeped in scripture such as Anthony De Mello,[6] an Indian Jesuit. In order to be healed of so much vacancy, so much fear of desiring anything, ACoA may, on the other hand, need to be encouraged to pray *with* their senses, not numbing or denying their looking, listening, touching. For example, contemplation of flowers, ocean waves, animals, children playing might enhance their contact with God, healing some fears of sensation and bodily appreciations. They might be guided to eat a meal alone, savoring every bite, learning to "taste and see" how good God is, how nourishing of hungry hearts.

Desire is the very stuff of Christian prayer, teaches St. Ignatius Loyola, whose spiritual exercises are classic. Jesus did not empty himself of desires. He wept with longing to gather the people of Jerusalem to himself, he yearned to eat a final meal with his friends. To be freed from attachments is an outcome of Ignatius' exercises, and ACoA do need to be freed by God from their addictions to persons, places and things. Desire, however, does not always mean inappropriate attachment, but can also mean a passionate movement of the heart toward what is good, helpful, healing, truly relational.

Adult children might be encouraged to use even more of their bodies when praying. Many of them have experienced parental abuse of their bodies and so fear or hate their bodies. In the privacy of their rooms, they might act out psalms with large body movements—for example, Psalm 23—"God spreads a table before me." Watch God spread the banquet. Seat yourself. Where do you sit in relation to God? How does it feel to be waited on by God? They might dance to records or tapes of psalms, hymns or sacred songs. Even kneeling, prostrating or standing with arms uplifted might offer some healing as the body becomes part of prayer. They might sing. As St. Augustine taught, singing is twice praying. The vocal cords, the emotional response which music stirs, even imperceptible movements which may accompany song offer more of the body to God.

Scriptural Prayer

Scriptural prayer can be helpful to ACoA. The psalms with their range and intensity of emotion[7] can give permission for the adult child to be himself or herself before God. Psalms can start juice flowing in a prayer life which feels like an arid desert. Psalms can permeate a day. For example, using the favorite "The Lord is my shepherd" psalm, ACoA may be encouraged to bring their past pain and present hurts and hopes to God.

Ps 23   What are the things which block your response to life, to people, to God? Ask the Lord to reveal these blocks—fears, hostilities, hurts, etc. Then repeat slowly: "I fear no evil for you are with me." You might repeat this verse all day long.

Ps 23   When has your response to life, your relationships with people and with God been most satisfying? Ask the Lord to reveal these happy or peaceful times to you. Repeat slowly: "Surely goodness and kindness shall follow me all the days of my life."

Psalms teach us that God knows us and loves us just the way we are. Psalm 103, which is about God's forgiveness and acceptance of our frailty, also proclaims that when we "bless" God, we hand over our life just as it is to our higher power.

Ps 103   If your translation reads "praise" change it to "bless," the original Hebrew word. Blessing someone means to exchange life with that person. To bless the Lord is to offer God your life. Note that this psalm deals with sin, and yet we offer a sinful life to God, for our creator surely knows that we are dust. Offer God the things about yourself which you really do not like.[8]

The variety of ways which the friends of God related to the Lord can give ACoA permission to be real in relationship: Abraham bargained, Sarah laughed, Jacob wrestled, Moses tried to shirk leadership, Miriam danced to tambourines, and so forth. Zacchaeus climbed a tree, Martha fixed supper, Mary of Bethany wept, Mary of Nazareth questioned, and Peter constantly made a fool of himself!

Scriptural prayer not only gives us permission to be who we are and to be loved as we are, it uses two of our sometimes forgotten internal senses: memory and imagination. Memory and hope might sum up the experience of the covenanted people who wrote the Jewish scriptures. Over and over again, on almost every page, they tell, sing, shout, wonder at, give thanks for God's great act on their behalf, God's freeing them from slavery. To remember, for the Jews and for Jesus, is to make present again. "Do this in memory of me" brings back Jesus' own action of thanking, blessing and giving. Remembering God's giving in the past deepens hope for God's saving in the future.

For example, Psalm 107 details a variety of ways in which God responded when people called out in distress. Some of those ways might still fit today's people of God. The stanza, for example, about being storm-tossed, losing strength and skill, would undoubtedly match the interior turbulence of some adult children.

Ps 107   When in your life have you been lost, hungry, thirsty? When have you been bound in chains or subdued in spirit? When have you been rebellious, repentant and healed? When have you been carried up to heaven and plunged into the depths? When have you been in deserts and when have you found a home? And how have you felt about the Lord during all these times? How do you feel about God as you remember your own salvation history?[9]

Imagination plays an important role in scriptural prayer because the Bible is laden with images, not abstract theories or doctrines. The gospel could have been set forth as credal statements but it never would have touched and transformed our whole being. Gospel is story and so engages us on many levels, inviting us to participate in the living, dying and rising of Jesus. The evangelists' imagination calls to our imagination to become involved with Jesus who still lives and works when we make his word our home.

For example, adult children might be invited to share their fears with Jesus in the garden of Gethsemane.

Lk 22:42–44   Look at Jesus, feel with Jesus in this experience of anxiety before his suffering. In looking at him, try to use as many of your senses as you can—can you hear the trees in the garden rustling, can you feel the wind, can you smell the fresh crispness of the night? In feeling with him, let your own anxieties surface. What worries you, of what are you afraid, what do you dread? Let your stomach knot up, your head throb if need be. Share your emotions with Jesus. Then try to listen as he talks about his fears and try to comfort him, understand him (which is a comfort). Remember that contemplation is, simply, looking at Jesus, trying to be with him in his life, trying to feel his feelings. It is a way of letting him share his mind and his heart with us so that when we relate to the body of Christ, the church—Christ's community of today—we may think his thoughts and love with his love.[10]

Intercession

If once we were taught that there were four kinds of prayer: adoration, thanksgiving, contrition and intercession, we now are assured that there are as many ways of being with God, addressing God as there are human personalities. Just for example, more of the one hundred and fifty psalms are laments than praise, thanksgiving and all other "types" combined. Laments, from the Hebrew *lamah* (why?), are simply complaints to God.

Sometimes intercession was ranked as a "lower form of prayer." This reinforced the ACoA sickness of not asking, not complaining, putting up with, de-selfing. How dare we bother God with our little needs or hopes? Of course adult children who put all their hope as children in God's rescuing them from alcoholic chaos, neglect and/or abuse will have a different and longer journey to learning to trust God again. Others did not ask God for anything because God could not possibly care. Those, however, who learned that intercession was "selfish" can look at Jesus' ministry right now. Hebrews states that Jesus stands before the face of God making intercession for us (Heb 7:25).

Jesus spends his risen life not praising or thanking but making intercession for us. Intercession is the way the Hebrew language describes prayer. To pray, in Hebrew, is to ask. The word means "to stroke the face of God." Jesus strokes the face of God on our behalf. For ACoA such intimacy might seem unbearable, so rather than insist that they try it, ask them to focus on Jesus—Jesus who asks, pleads for all their needs, intercedes on their behalf. Jesus will desire in their stead until they are ready to join his prayer.

Faith-Sharing Groups

A minister who listens to many parishioners who want to grow in relationship with God might structure faith-sharing groups. Such an experience might prove helpful to ACoA who, experience has taught, are healed best in group settings.

A weekly meeting, one to one and a half hours, might include some exercises such as these, which strike at all three restrictions of an alcoholic family. Here ACoA are encouraged to feel, to talk and gradually to trust.

Open the group with a prayer to the Spirit. Allow five minutes of silence to remember and to get in touch with the various emotions of the week. Ask participants to choose a psalm from the category that describes their feeling-tone. Allow another five minutes to read/pray the psalm silently. Invite them to share their feelings and those parts of the psalm which express how they feel right now.
Praises: Psalms 8, 78, 104, 105, 117, 135, 150

Laments: Psalms 22, 42, 43, 51, 71, 80
Thanks: Psalms 34, 66, 67, 75, 118, 138
Curses: Psalms 35, 59, 69, 109, 137, 140

At another meeting, participants might name a favorite psalm and tell why it speaks to them. During the week they might rewrite a psalm in their own words. For example, Psalm 23: "The Lord is my leader. I am not afraid to move on when I can remember that God is in charge . . ." They can be encouraged to compose their own lament and to pray it with the group.

If personal feelings are too painful to share early-on, this kind of psalm sharing might focus on others' pain—for a while. For example, encourage the group to pay attention to the television news about a certain situation which they consider unjust. Invite participants to get inside the skin of the victims of this injustice and to write a prayer, even a cursing prayer, out of their skin. Let them share these modern cursing psalms at your next group meeting. If participants leave that meeting in tears or furious or discouraged, encourage them to give those powerful emotions to the Lord all the way home. Ask God to channel the energy of that emotion into positive action, however small, for justice here or abroad.[11]

It is important to remember when faith-sharing that no verbal comment is allowed. This withholding of verbal judgment, even when complimentary, gradually weans participants away from making any kind of mental judgment on the worth of a person's contribution. These judgments spring from comparison, a trap for ACoA, hungering not just for acceptance and approval but even just to be considered "normal," like everybody else. The "no verbal comment" rule then gradually eliminates comparisons (and many ACoA do tend to compare themselves less favorably). Then their own receptivity to God at work so uniquely in the other's life can grow. The rule also teaches participants to use their bodies: eye contact, facial expression, relaxation, to communicate openness and a listening with the heart.

Chapter 13

Spiritual Direction

Elements of spiritual direction may resemble friendship, confession, faith-sharing, guidance in prayer, and/or pastoral counseling. Friendship must be mutual and friends are expected to become emotionally involved in each other's lives. A spiritual director does not seek mutual support in the spiritual journey nor does he or she become emotionally involved. A director offers a form of pastoral care which requires some objectivity for the sake of clarity.

A confessor probes for roots of sin. While a director might help a person uncover sin, the emphasis in direction is more on discovering grace. One who comes for direction needs, like a participant in a faith-sharing group, to be able to articulate faith, that is, the growing attachment and commitment to Christ and to articulate the ways in which Christ's Spirit is leading. There are, however, many more goals in direction, and, unlike faith-sharing, the director will comment, perhaps even confront. A request for guidance in prayer may lead eventually to direction but direction is not the place for teaching.

Pastoral counseling and direction share many of the same dynamics such as a therapeutic relationship, transference, countertransference, resistance. Yet pastoral counseling chiefly focuses on the person in his or her human relationships whether past or present, strategizing ways to help clients relate more freely and lovingly. While spiritual direction may lead to the same outcome, the focus is on the person's relationship with God/Jesus/Spirit.

By spiritual direction we mean that form of pastoral care in which one person seeks a facilitator for his or her spiritual development as they examine together the Spirit's leading and transforming of the person. The Spirit is the one, true director of anyone's spiritual journey. The director is a companion on that journey. The direction is the Spirit's and the person's own; a spiritual director acts more like a reflector, mirroring back to the person what that person feels, thinks, wants, chooses in living the life of the Spirit.

People seek a spiritual director for a variety of reasons. Some Christians may seek direction because, all unprepared, they have powerfully experienced a conversion, a deep spiritual touch, a taste of and for God. They come to unpack that extraordinary experience with a minister trained in the spiritual life; they want to understand the meaning of it, the call inherent in it, the power, energy, or fear to which it gives birth.

Most Christians come with more ordinary experiences, hopes and goals: to develop a contemplative attitude; to search out why prayer or their relationship with God feels so blocked; to grow in habits of discernment or to discern a major decision; to facilitate the Spirit's transformation of their daily living, loving, working. They come wanting to know and love God more intimately. They are eager to grow in wisdom and grace.

Some come for less appropriate reasons, yet need not be turned away if the director can be clear. Some come, for example, really needing counseling or therapy. It is important that the spiritual director assert periodically that he or she is not trained to do pastoral counseling, but with that warning, and with periodic offers to make a referral, the director can listen and let the relationship build—at the person's own pace. After trust develops between the person and director, the person may only then accept a referral to a mental health professional but also can be invited to continue the direction relationship concomitantly with the therapy.

Some come, especially professed religious, priests, and ministers, so that the director may hold them accountable for their spiritual life. This is not a growthful foundation for a direction relationship and needs to be discussed at once. The "lost children" and "placators" of the dysfunctional home may be too quick to share responsibility for their spiritual growth. The "heroes" may be frightened that things will fall apart if someone else does not help control the Spirit's movement.

ACoA, or those working any Twelve Step program, may look for a director who understands and appreciates the spirituality of the program. Some "get stuck" at the second step which acknowledges the higher power's desire to save, or the third, a major act of trust in handing over control of one's will and entire life to God. Some come when they reach the eleventh step, actively seeking through prayer and meditation to know and relate more deeply with their higher power.

To understand and appreciate Twelve Step spirituality means a director does not try to get the person to take control of his or her addiction. That hope may be appropriate if the person is not in a Twelve Step program and resists beginning it. To encourage a "lost child" type of ACoA to choose more autonomy and freedom, to assume more responsibility for his or her own life, too, might be appropriate. ACoA who are the heroes, however, or those working the Twelve Steps, need encouragement in handing over to God for healing their past life and pain, their current need for forgiveness, reconciliation and integration.

While important in all direction relationships, perhaps most essential for the director working with someone in recovery is a non-directive approach. Encouragement in letting go and letting God, reminders that God only gives us one day at a time, mirroring back the person's desire to let God save, to let God be God, can be helpful. Nor is this approach new or foreign to classical spiritual journeys. The "principle and foundation" of Ignatius' spiritual exercises, for example, so true for four hundred years, states bluntly that God is God and we are creatures, limited, sinful and incredibly loved. When a person being directed in the spiritual exercises grasps that principle experientially, and only then, will a skilled director let the person proceed with the Ignatian exercises.

Not only do the ACoA and the director share a need to let God be God of this relationship, the director must keep alert to any toxic ways which trouble it. For example, because an ACoA needs to control reality, he or she may try to manipulate the director. Because boundaries in an alcoholic family are loose, an ACoA may claim too much time, may introduce important topics at the last minute so as to run over the "fifty minute hour," may inappropriately phone, or write long letters to the director between sessions. Instead of keeping annoyance, even anger, a secret in the relationship, a director needs directly to reestablish boundaries at the next session. On the other hand, the director should be prepared, because the ACoA's ability to trust may be so damaged, to allow the therapeutic relationship to take much longer to build. Especially, the director must not push insights or probe past pain which can tear down the ACoA's defenses. The Spirit will lead the ACoA to truth gradually and appropriately.

The Powerful Religious Experience

Let us return to the initial reasons which spur people to spiritual direction and see how they might lead to or reinforce healing for adult children. First, the powerful religious experience. ACoA tend to have numbed their senses, feelings and desires in order to survive the traumas of growing up. It is no wonder then that some of them need a "breakthrough," a way for the Spirit to surprise them into recognition of God's unconditional love, or Jesus' personal choice of them, or the Spirit's flaming in the depths of their being.

Their senses may throb, their sexuality may surge, their own tenderness or fear or joy may melt them, overwhelm them. Who could understand, reassure them, take their experience seriously and perhaps tell them it is not all illusion, hysteria or even indigestion? They turn to a spiritual director. They need, desperately sometimes, to talk, to trust their experience, their God. They need to know that their senses and emotions are not sinful. They need to know that they are normal. They need to unpack the meaning of this breakthrough gradually and in calmer times. So they begin the process of spiritual direction which may well indeed be part of the process of God's healing the adult child.

One woman in her early thirties describes such a process which began after she had faithfully attended Overeaters Anonymous meetings for some time. Returning to her car after a meeting, she sat in the dark and felt a "higher power" move in her heart. She had been reared an agnostic but sought out an evangelical minister later in the week who prayed with her. He invited her to baptism right then and there. As he laid hands on her head she felt what she described as a "backward blush." It felt as though a demon were leaving her, and inside she had turned scarlet, scrubbed new and fresh.

Two years later, the woman asked to begin spiritual direction. She had no church affiliation but was ready, she surmised, to find community not only with her Overeaters Anonymous group but in the community of Christ. She had been reading theology voraciously and now wanted a companion on her journey, not so much to God who was, she felt, constantly companioning her, but to a community, to involvement and ministry within it.

A Contemplative Attitude

At times ACoA who do not turn to substances to escape try to escape into prayer. We hear of one minister who left his wife to suffer alone through her first childbirthing because "God" had called him to a solitary retreat. Burned out priests, workaholic sisters, may claim a call to a monastery or cloister. The hermetical or contemplative life can be an escape from community, work, responsibility, and, for the para-alcoholic, can look so holy.

All Christians are called to a contemplative attitude, however, an integration of prayer, love and work, a receptivity to the wonders, joys and sorrows of each day. Spiritual direction, through regular sharing of faith with a single director or in a group, can enhance the contemplative attitude.

Mary, the mother of Jesus, "pondered all these things in her heart." Even more a model than Jesus, who got away now and then to a lonely place, Mary as woman, wife and mother could not leave Nazareth for a night on a mountaintop. She was open, in her contemplative attitude, to hear angels, kinswoman, and Simeon; she was also receptive to smelly, boisterous shepherds and could treasure their words, too, in her heart.

Contemplatives are simply those sensitive women and men, very much immersed in the world, who are alert to hear God's word, to see God's action, to feel God's nudge. They are lifted out of themselves to enter the world of another by listening compassionately. They transcend their self-centeredness to see and respond to the needs of others. They experience the mystery of God in a variety of events and give thanks. Contemplatives live "an attitude of gratitude." They not only find God in all things but they are eager to let God find them, reveal to them, love them in every situation. It is this growing awareness, receptivity, self-transcendence, mutuality with God which they talk about in direction.

A seventy year old teaching brother came for spiritual direction, so discouraged to be ending his days without a very robust spiritual life. What had he done wrong, was there any hope? He had, ever so many years ago, left an alcoholic mother to join a community which was quite cloistered. With the renewal of his congregation after Vatican II, he too became more apostolic than monastic in outlook, but the result tended to be a nodding off during his hour of solitary contemplation each morning.

His director, instead of focusing on his discouraging one hour of prayer, asked about his relationship with God. "We're fine together," he smiled. "He goes with me as I do my home-visiting and I surely couldn't say such wise words to my patients if he were not in my heart and on my lips." His director marveled. This man had begun, at seventy, to use his retirement from teaching to be a hospice volunteer, traveling alone through a rural county in heat and snow, to comfort the dying—yet not alone. God and he were companions, co-ministers, friends. Without knowing it, his "God-talk" was so integrated in his life that he was even paraphrasing scripture: "in my heart and on my lips" describes his openness to God.

This hospice volunteer and his director have met once a month for two years now. It is still difficult for this adult child not to perform well during prayer time. He was asked recently, however, to take on a different, more administrative kind of ministry, to be the superior in the brothers' retirement community. His discernment hinged on which job would lead him to an ever deepening awe in God's presence, at God's action. "No doubt about it," he stated firmly. "I'm not going to get hooked on which group of people needs me more. I'm going to stay right here where God is filling everything all day long. Except my hour of prayer!"

Self-transcendence in the presence of mystery happens. It can not be produced. It can be prepared for by working through the adult child's denial of senses, feelings, humanity. One needs first a sensing, feeling, human self before one can transcend. Directors can reinforce an incarnational kind of prayer, rooted in the flesh (*carne* in Latin). One director asks a new directee to spend a day contemplating water; another day, listening first to a favorite piece of music, then to a jarring piece; to smell and touch and taste a favorite food over the course of an hour. Practices such as these can help open an adult child to the surrounding world. A very damaged incest survivor who hated God as an abusive father discovered a new higher power/ deeper energy by using St. Augustine's name for God: "Oh, Beauty, ever ancient, ever new. Late have I loved you, yet never have I loved till now." "Beauty" gave this artistically gifted man a new name, new image of God who communicates through the glory of nature and art.

A practice which fosters a contemplative attitude is a daily examination of consciousness. This might be recorded in a journal and articulated with a director. Since the major movement of Christian living is the sharing of Jesus' dying and rising (the core of baptism, eucharist and New Testament), directors might encourage the noticing of dying experiences each day—worries, hurts, angers, disappointments, etc.—and rising experiences—a long-distance call, a word of praise, a lucky bus connection, a favorite meal, a good talk with one's teenager.

Some other approaches to building a habit of noticing, paying attention to God in daily living might be to record where sin was during each day, and where grace was. Another: What was God teaching me (discipleship) today? in the joys? in the sorrows? in my feeling-responses? A third: Where was God at work today in my life? What was God doing? How was God setting me free? Another: What has been the good news in my life today?

Another, based on the AA Serenity Prayer: When was I serene and trusting? When was I courageous? When was I wise today? These last questions may lead to prayers of gratitude.

Blocks to Relationship

Blocks to relationship with God push some people to spiritual direction. They feel frustrated by prayer to a God who seems distant. General irritation begins to flood their day. Life itself is gradually becoming a desert. There are books written about obstacles to prayer, dark nights and other frightening clues to one's advancing in the spiritual life. ACoA get trapped by advancing, measuring, taking their spiritual pulse. It seems more healing to stay with experiences from scripture in which, apart from Jesus and Mary perhaps, people are not ranked according to how advanced they are in relationship with God.

Nor does the God of scripture withhold love and fidelity in order to "test" our love. What an insecure God that would be! God does not get into competition with our human loves, demanding to be first in our affections. Adult children may have simply projected onto God our own co-dependent insecurities and think that God competes for our hearts. Instead, God is, in hearts which are healing, the very bond between us and our loves. A director may then have to help ACoA discern true love of God from a projection of co-dependency onto God.

ACoA are unusually guilt-laden, fear-ridden and/or furious in often repressed ways. Some major blocks to relationship in our human loving are isolation, infidelity, fear, anger. Our most significant human relationships usually parallel our relationship with God.

Sometimes the guilt of adult children is unfounded, and at times it stems from real sin: infidelity to God's love or isolation from people. Sin blocks our spiritual life. Again, there is a trap for ACoA who accuse themselves so often, so falsely. The remedy is to ask God, in prayer, to reveal sin in our lives. When people feel that God is distant, a director can ask them to pray daily for God to show them their sin, to help them not to deny truth, not to rationalize.

They are not allowed to examine their consciences. ACoA are

so adept at scraping their spirit raw, looking for even more sin. God's revelation of sin to us, however, is a peace-filled process. "Go call your husband," Jesus invites the Samaritan woman. "I have no husband." "You have spoken truly . . ." (Jn 4:16–18). Jesus does not condemn. He reveals and the woman responds with energy, in mission.

Sometimes the sin which Jesus reveals is quite different from our own conception. He can penetrate our hearts more deeply and can wean us from the denial we often use as a defense against the truth of our real sin. For example, countless ACoA obsess about sex. All sin is distilled into sex. Sexual feelings, desires, acting out become distorted as the cycle of shame leads to even more obsessive-compulsive addictions to sex. When Jesus reveals sin, he is likely to bypass sex altogether. There is so much injustice, oppression, violence, hatred in our world but we have our eyes fixed firmly on every twitch of genitalia! There is less energy for our mission of justice and love when so much energy is consumed by labeling, measuring, judging those twitches, and lugging the subsequent guilt. We lay burdens on our own backs!

Fear of or addiction to sex often is linked with alcohol; for example, parents may have become affectionate, sentimental, even incestuous when drinking. Adult children then may use alcohol to block their fear and shame of sex and thus act inappropriately while drinking. Even within marriage, ACoA may need alcohol to become unrestrained and amorous. Or they may black out so as to avoid sexual intimacy. Sex and Love Addicts Anonymous (SLAA) offers a Twelve Step program and a community of healing. Like the Samaritan woman with her five husbands, there is no need to be ashamed when Jesus reveals addiction.

A second block to relationship is fear. ACoA are afraid of intimacy and so a closeness with God can be frightening. In human loves, ACoA are often afraid of being rejected and/or abandoned and so hide what they judge to be less acceptable aspects of themselves. With God, the fear seems most often to center on what God will ask, require, demand.

"I don't want to get too close to God, because look what God did to Jesus" is a refrain often heard by those who offer directed retreats. In a directed as opposed to a preached retreat, the retreatant may spend an entire day of prayer with just a few verses of scripture. Such a focused experience allows persons to plumb unknown depths of their relationship with God. Often God reveals them to themselves as well. Mystery, intimacy are so overwhelming, so retreatants visit a spiritual director each day, to ponder the depths with an experienced companion. In such an experience, it is hard to hide.

What does God ask? God's will, desire is our healing, wholeness, peace. God will not intrude on our privacy, however, if we decide to hide parts of ourselves. Once the Lord has invited us to closeness, God waits to be invited in return. God can wait a lifetime, in respect for our freedom, our timing. What does God require, demand? Only unhealthy love makes demands. How could God's love ever want our crucifixion? These are important areas for a spiritual director to explore in order to facilitate God's freeing from fear.

Anger which is repressed is a common block in our human relationships. If anger is stored up, it can explode inappropriately and almost devastate its recipient. If anger trickles out, passive-aggressive behaviors and bitter attitudes can prevail.[1] So with God, our anger can be skewed.

People say "Why blame God?" or "How dare I lift my fist to God?" or "God knows best." Again scripture portrays the friends of God arguing with God (Gen 18:17–33), complaining incessantly (Ps 13 et al.), feeling betrayed (Jer 20:7), wrestling with God (Gen 32:23–31). God of the scriptures invites us to express just how we are. Then we know our feelings and God knows how we feel as well. God needs to hear our disappointments, frustrations, angers and rages at life, even at God, for God will not mind-read or feeling-read, intruding on our privacy (as many parents in alcoholic families did).

Logic, some people argue, precludes our blaming God. This pain, loss, etc. is due to human freedom. God has nothing to do with it. Friends often use each other as sounding boards for their anger. For example, a wife has been unfairly treated at the office and stomps into the house, yelling at her husband, "Do you know what John said to me today?" Only with those we trust can we dare let our anger out. A flare-up at a store clerk does not leave us vulnerable. On the other hand, a pouring out to a friend of fury at an injustice leaves us helpless, shaking—and more free. Anger shared with God or even anger at God can be an act of trust, of intimacy, leave us closer to each other.

There is one form of anger, however, which undercuts ACoA healing. The attitude of gratitude can be eroded by an anger which springs from a sense of entitlement. For example, the flare-up at the store clerk implies that I am deserving of all attention immediately. Entitlement can be an addiction and can easily infiltrate our relationship with God. "I deserve better than this from God" is the cry of a deprived child. "Deserve?" Unfortunately, even the followers of Martin Luther who demonstrated theologically again and again that we deserve nothing from God, that all is grace, have sometimes forgotten that basic tenet of the scriptures. It is not by our works that we are saved, loved. It is God's free gift of grace in the beloved, not any reward for works accomplished (Eph 2:8–9).

How can a director facilitate the unblocked response to God's gifts of grace, God's initiative and invitation to intimacy? Primarily, the removal of blocks is like the removal of addiction. After admission of powerlessness, the blocked person needs to hand over the struggle to Jesus who is strong to save.

An image of Jesus may help. In John 7:37–39, Jesus promises a fountain of living water flowing from deep within us. He was speaking of the Spirit, source of our spiritual life. Although a huge boulder lands on top of that living spring, water can seep out from under it; no one can squelch the Spirit. In imagination, Jesus puts his arms around that boulder: sin, fear, anger, undoubtedly others as well. Note, Jesus does not dynamite the block; we sometimes in our impatience to pluck out sin or rush through fear and anger might be destructive. Instead, Jesus embraces the block, then heaves it aside. To embrace our fear or anger, to notice where in our sin grace even more abounded, is to be able more freely to let it go. The director can pray with the blocked person for Jesus to enable the living water to flow again.

Discernment

". . . the wisdom to know the difference." A prime purpose for seeking spiritual direction is to discern. Some view discernment as a process of prudent decision-making, but there is a more total growth in wisdom available, even as one grows in grace. Because ACoA can be compulsive about being right, a director may have to broaden the framework, from making a major decision to a whole way of life, one which accords well with the Twelve Steps.

Adult children have grown up in a milieu of what AA calls "stinkin' thinkin'." In our professionalism, we might term it "cognitive disorder." The whole family was affected by the alcoholic's crooked thinking, with the children undoubtedly learning imprudent and unwise ways to view and evaluate life.

For someone who wants spiritual direction in order to live a life of discernment, "Bill," AA's co-founder, explains how to do it in simple words: "I was to test my thinking by the new God-consciousness within."[2] That new or renewed God-consciousness may first of all cut through decades of denial, denial of reality, truth, experience, self. It unmasks the adult child, but because God/Jesus/Spirit do the unmasking, the movement will probably be slow, somewhat imperceptible to the person. The objective director may be able to perceive the fruits of growing in truth and wisdom and can helpfully feed back what he or she, in a contemplative attitude toward the directee, has noticed.

Discerning truth leads to wisdom and freedom. It cuts away at repression so that gradually all of living and loving may be brought into the light of Christ. John's community talks about those who prefer the darkness, but they are usually not those who choose regular sessions with a director.

Some want to "discern God's will" in a major decision. Often, through prayer to know what God wants, adult children are surprised, sometimes frightened to discover that God often wants what they want. "In their distress they called to the Lord and God brought them (sailors on a turbulent sea) straight to the port which they wanted" (Ps 107:30). A director may patiently have to reassure adult children, asking them to trust their own experience of prayer.

Some ACoA, in making a decision, however, have scant idea of what they themselves want. Then a director can offer questions for them to pray with such as: Which choice will lead to more life? which to a deeper, healthier, happier life? "Choose life!" God urges us through Moses. That call (Dt 30:19) may at first confuse and frighten adult children who expect so much death from their decisions, perhaps even expect God to command: "Choose pain, choose the hardest thing, choose death."

Another guiding suggestion might be to have the person imagine himself or herself in each one of the choices (marriage, or job, or city, etc.). In imagination, which situation provides more growth in love, joy, peace, patience, kindness, generosity, faithfulness, gentleness and self-control? These are the fruits of the Spirit (Gal 5:22–23), not virtues which we can produce by making correct decisions. Rather they flower when our life is directed by the Spirit, as St. Paul observed from his own experience. Notice, self-control is not a virtue which we practice, although many ACoA have made it a cardinal virtue. Self-control as a fruit of the Spirit is the Spirit's gift. The Spirit leads to freedom, not to control. Instead of reinforcing stoic notions of self-control, second nature to ACoA, the Spirit teaches us to take responsibility for our life. That is the self-control, or authority within the self, which the Spirit alone can produce.

Leading a life directed by the Spirit, a life of discernment of what God wants, fosters a connaturality with God. Just as a husband knows intuitively after many years of life together what will please his wife, just as a wife can almost without thinking choose a gift for her husband because she knows his tastes,[3] so can a relationship with God become so deep and natural that one thinks with the mind of God, loves with the heart of God. "It's second nature to me now," and the song continues, "like breathing out and breathing in." There is no need for the furrowed brow, the soul-searching, the drama or the chaos which attract some ACoA in their seeking to "do God's will."

If God has a will! The scriptures sometimes would make us think that God has a heavenly blueprint which we must work hard to discover so that we do everything right, correctly, even perfectly. Sometimes scripture is consoling, like God's plans for us, according to Jeremiah:

> I know the plans I have in mind for you . . . plans for peace, not disaster, reserving a future full of hope for you. Then when you call to me and come to plead with me, I will listen to you. When you seek me with all your heart, I will let you find me (Jer 29:11–14).

Other times it seems that God's plan is a "should" which indeed leads to disaster. "Was it not necessary that the Messiah should suffer these things . . . ?" (Lk 24:26). Suppose God, respecting our freedom, has no plan? Suppose God, with a contemplative attitude, stands in awe and wonder at how we grow and love and think and choose? God surely must, like any good parent (and there's the rub for the ACoA), have strong desires for our health and happiness. What parent, however, can control exactly how a child will grow? What parent, if healthy, would want to control an adult child? What healthy parent so structures an adult child's life that there can be no choice, no freedom, no mistakes? And what healthy adult child allows a parent so to control?

"Healthy" is the operative word. ACoA have not known healthy parental love, healthy parental authority. A chief discernment for the adult child then, who, like "Bill," wants to test his or her thinking by a God-consciousness, even connaturality with God, will be in the areas of love vs. co-dependency, obedience vs. conformity. A director who is familiar enough with the pathology of co-dependence, who is alert to subservience, and who is clear, can help ACoA explore an adult morality based on true love of God, self and others, on authentic obedience to God and to reality.

Lifelong Transformation

In Galatians, Paul writes about the tension between the Spirit and the flesh. He summarizes his previous argument against Christians' living a life under the law: "If you are guided by the Spirit, you are not under the law" (Gal 5:18). It is hard for adult children who grew up in chaos not to seek some kind of security, even when it becomes slavery. Paul exhorts: "For freedom Christ has set us free. Stand firm and never submit to any kind of slavery" (Gal 5:1).

Some adult children are ruled by the flesh, and most think that means sex alone. Paul lists the fruits of the flesh, however: "immorality, impurity, licentiousness, idolatry, sorcery, hatreds, rivalry, jealousy, outbursts of fury, acts of selfishness, dissensions, factions, envy, drinking bouts, orgies and the like" (Gal 5:19–21). Notice that while fleshly, bodily sins are included, so are sins of the mind. For Paul, flesh means much more than the body. Flesh is a sphere of influence, a reign of darkness within us which wars against the Spirit. Paul might envision Christian living as the gradual transformation of the flesh by the action of God's Spirit. Gradually the dark and enslaved parts of us are brought into the light of Christ, into the freedom of the Spirit.

> The Lord is the Spirit. Where the Spirit of the Lord is, there is freedom. All of us, gazing . . . on the glory of the Lord, are being transformed into the image of Christ, from glory to glory. Such is the influence of the Lord who is the Spirit (2 Cor 3:17–18).

Glory is a biblical word which connotes light and splendor. Coming into the light of Christ is in itself a healing, a transforming of years of ACoA denial, family secrets, obsessive-compulsiveness which is slavery. The transformation is not merely into freedom. We are transformed into the image of the glory-filled Christ. Such is the influence (from the Latin for the "flowing into") of the Spirit.

No wonder then that in his letter to the Galatians where Paul wrestles with the tensions between law and freedom, between flesh and Spirit, he describes his discipleship as em-bodi-ment of Christ.

"It is no longer I who live, but Christ lives within me" (Gal 2:20). A director can facilitate the growing likeness to Christ, into Christ.

Like Christ, the adult child will grow in wisdom, knowing God, God's mind and heart, God's desires and choices, God's loves and hates. Like Christ, the adult child will grow in age, in becoming more fully human, rightfully appropriating all aspects of the humanity fully alive which is God's glory (St. Irenaeus). Like Christ, the adult child will grow in grace, living the life in abundance of God. With the Spirit's direction and influence, there is hope for healing and wholeness. A spiritual director is blessed to observe the growth, to speak the timely word of God, to wonder in gratitude at the lifelong transformation of each directee.

Chapter 14

Other One-on-One Service

The forms of ministry already treated—liturgical leadership, preaching, teaching, crisis intervention, pastoral counseling and spiritual direction—are usually offered by trained professionals. However, whether as deacon, sexton or elder, whether in a variety of new lay ministries emerging in Roman Catholic parishes, many volunteers and semi-professionals build up the local community with their service to individuals and their families. For example, if much of society seems to abandon the elderly, the churches have appreciated the needs of the shut-ins and those in nursing homes. The hospitalized can usually count on a visit from a designated representative of their church, as can those grieving a death in the family.

Every Christian who visits, prays with, grieves with even his or her own family members and friends is exercising gifts of service for the building up of community. For those volunteers, however, who do represent their congregations in a designated service, we offer the following suggestions for listening to those shut-ins, hospitalized, grieving or elderly who may be adult children. We will focus on the elderly as a case in point.

Sometimes an ordained or lay minister brings communion to a shut-in or leads the rosary in a nursing home. Yet it is listening which embodies the Lord's love, so many report. In listening to the elderly tell their story, share their memories, the attentive listener is helping an integrating process which is often healing as well as wholing. There is no need for the listening minister to ask probing questions or make interpretations. Something happens deep within the teller as he or she hears the reality spoken out loud to a respectful, responsive listener. As we have seen with pastoral counseling and spiritual direction, it may take a very long time to build a relationship of trust in which darker secrets and shameful fears may be spoken.

The elderly especially may have moral judgments on alcoholics and their behavior, judgments which may compound "the family secret." Their generation of preachers bewailed and harangued about alcohol from the pulpit. They lived through times of prohibition and temperance leagues. Their society reinforced the immorality of using alcohol, let alone its abuse.

It is not necessary for the enlightened minister to convince anyone that alcoholism is a disease nor to foist the latest ACoA book off on anyone. With the elderly who are often trying to make sense of their lives and peace with themselves, their families and God, it may be more helpful for a minister to focus on forgiveness of the alcoholic (be that parent, for the elderly often return emotionally to "live" in memory with their parents; be that self as alcoholic; be that spouse, child or grandchild). One thing usually which we can all agree on is that alcoholism is a terrible evil. No need to argue further.

If the elderly have problems with a God who does not rescue from evil or wipe out alcoholism, it is important to address this area of theology—but again, more by listening than teaching. A comment like, "Yes, it really is hard to understand why God allows alcoholism to continue," paraphrasing their own remark, may stimulate them to reflect further. If the person gets stuck, repetitive, a question like "I wonder why God just doesn't put a stop to it?" may get them probing their own faith. "While all this abuse was happening, how were you and God? Did God seem far away or close? loving or cruel or just absent?" Questions like these lead, hopefully, to more memories, more stories.

If the ordained find they have time only for quick prayers with or over the elderly and the shut-ins, perhaps a hasty communion service, a congregation may do well to enlist laity who have listening skills in this important healing ministry. It is never too late for healing. St. Augustine writes: "Despair of no one so long as he [or she] lives." Healing is God's work. *Shalom*, the Hebrew for peace but which also means wholeness and integration, is God's gift, especially, as Erik Erikson teaches, for the elderly.

A Final Hope for Professionals and Volunteers

Whether volunteer or professional, ordained or lay, ministers can always be strengthened, their skills sharpened by support groups or even peer supervision sponsored by the congregation or among congregations. While confidentiality of conversations and situations must be preserved, there are ways to conceal names or other identifying details in reflecting on and sharing a pastoral visit.

Theological reflection, well analyzed in an abundance of books used in seminary, may be simplified by a pastor who periodically yet regularly calls together the parish staff or parish volunteers. A question such as "Where do you find grace at work in this ministry—or this situation—or this case (if a case is being detailed)?" may be enough. If the ministers tend to co-dependency, the reflection/sharing might be facilitated by asking them to record their feelings in a journal after each pastoral encounter. Then the question in the group might be: What feelings blocked your ministry and what feelings were grace for you?

We need support in our ministry. Some unrecovering ACoA ministers of the family hero type may want to "go it alone," or of the "lost child" type may fear sharing in groups. Surely, however, one of the blessings of the ACoA movement is to reassure us that we who serve and lead the church community can grow ever more free from the messiah complexes, slights, jealousies, competitions, which burn us out when we act out of unhealed needs and hungers. That we may be one, *as* the Father and Jesus are one, that the world may know God sent him!

Chapter 15

Prayer

To conclude this section on the ministry to ACoA, we focus on prayer as both a public and personal form of building up the community. In season and out, when sick or retired or on vacation, the minister can pray. "Whatever we do in word or in work, we do everything in the name of Jesus" (Col 3:17). Our ministry continues the healing work of Jesus among his people, and includes, as his did, prayer. Jesus, our priest, our minister, spends his risen life making intercession for us (Heb 7:25). We join him, interceding for our congregations, our adult children and their families.

We can use images in our intercession. We can lift up those individuals and families in need of healing, picturing ourselves handing them over to Jesus, or together with Jesus, laying our hands on them. We can imagine ourselves anointing them with the name of Jesus. Imaging the word, the name "Jesus," in solid gold letters above the head of the person or family, we can watch the name melt, and drench those for whom we pray. "Your name is like oil poured out" (Song 1:3).

We can imagine the Holy Spirit in our intercessory prayer. Watching the Spirit's fire light up from the inside or the Spirit's breath caress their faces, we can pray for our wounded ones. We can beg the Spirit to light, to fire, to caress, "to warm the frozen, melt the chill" (from the ancient sequence, "Veni Creator") and picture the Spirit's energy and action on behalf of those we care for. We can send the Spirit to them.

Scripture provides so many ways to help our intercessory prayers become more graphic and tangible. For example, we can image God's or Jesus' hands open to receive, carved with the names of those for whom we pray. "I will never forget you, I have carved you on the palms of my hands" (Is 49:15–16). Believing the promise of Isaiah and John of Patmos, we might image our God drying the tears of our adult children and their families. We can picture Jesus, in concrete detail, in technicolor and with sound track, kneeling at the

148

feet of each person to wash his or her feet, his or her pain. Sometimes these images, because they engage more of our humanness, provoke more fervor in us than just a list of folk on whose behalf we say words of petition.

Psalms are prayers easily adapted to painful situations. Many of the laments are either the sighs of the sick or the cries of the falsely accused. Adult children can relate to both categories. We might pray these laments in their name, or pray together with them before or after pastoral visits. One woman protested that she did not feel right complaining to God. Yet she often used psalms in her prayer. "What does 'in my distress I cried to the Lord' mean to you?" her minister asked her. "Oh!" Lights came on in her eyes as words simply recited before became real for her in *her* distress.

Before praying these psalms with ACoA, however, we may have to edit the laments. Laments consistently end with gratitude. God has paid attention. Our adult children may not have experienced God's response to them yet, and do not need God's "silence" exacerbated. When we pray alone, however, as Jesus prayed in gratitude even before he called Lazarus out of the tomb, we can end the lament with trust and gratitude, certain of God's faithful love.

Finally, we might pray in solidarity with all those involved in the process of healing. The prayer of noted theologian Reinhold Niebuhr, is used by AA and its offspring programs.

God, grant me the
   Serenity to accept the things
      I cannot change;

Courage to change the things I
      can; and
   Wisdom to know the difference.

Living one day at a time;
   Enjoying one moment at a time;
   Accepting hardship
      as the pathway to peace;

Taking as He did, this sinful
      world as it is, not as I would
      have it;

Trusting that He will make all
      things right if I surrender
      to His Will;

That I may be reasonably happy
in this life, and supremely
happy with Him forever in
the next. Amen.

Jesus embodied these three gifts of God—serenity, courage and wisdom. His serenity flowed from his trust, from his realization that he was a creature, limited, and that God was God. He depended on God alone and knew peace. His courage flowed from his inner authority, God's gift to him, that he might confront the injustices and suffering of his time. His wisdom flowed from his connaturality with God, his being so close to the mind and heart of God that he could decide and/or accept wisely. We might pray this prayer with him and in union with all those in recovery.

We pray, not to change God's mind or heart, not to bring down God's love and fidelity. God heals and saves without our prayer. We pray so that our compassion might both deepen and broaden, our contemplation might make us more attentive to God and others. We pray, from the Hebrew "ask" which means literally "to stroke the face of God." We come very close to God indeed.

PART V

The Church as a System

"Jesus died to gather all the scattered children of God into one family" (Jn 11:52). The image of church as family is very ancient. In modern times, Martin Luther like Jesus wanted no man called father; one of his reforms was certainly to recast the authoritarian family model of church in such a way that his twentieth century disciple, Dietrich Bonhoeffer, could write of Christians come of age. Yet there are ways in which all Christian denominations undoubtedly perpetuate the authority of the paterfamilias over the "little ones," the faithful "children." We need to reimage church so as to begin to renew some church structures.

We have titled this section "The Church as a System." System includes both participants and processes. Participants in church are people of God, are the body of Christ. Yet we are also community and organization. It would be neither fair nor accurate to dichotomize between laity and clergy, yet we the ordinary ministers are often the bridge between people and the highest human religious authority: bishop, convention, Vatican, etc.

In this section we will first focus on church as community of believers, a group which may operate as co-dependents. Second, we will pay attention to the church as organization which may be an "addictive substance." Then we shall note similarities between the church organization and the dysfunctional family. Finally we will issue some alerts to those in the institution who minister to ministers so that they may not unwittingly promote unhealthy learned behaviors in the ACoA whom they serve.

Each Christian denomination will undoubtedly play variations on these three themes. Ministers who already share ecumenical meetings might discuss this material and raise to awareness even more areas in which any part of the church/community/organization repeats unhealthy family patterns.

Chapter 16

The Church: Community of Believers and Co-Dependents

Throughout this book we have examined a variety of ways in which ministers might more effectively serve individual people who are ACoA. Let us summarize a few characteristics which a minister might unwittingly foster in his or her community if not alert to co-dependent behaviors and attitudes. Because many relate to the local church as family, pastors have an opportunity to provide new and healing structures for them.

The three cardinal rules for ACoA—do not feel, do not talk, do not trust—are so fundamental that they must lead this list of summary statements about co-dependent issues. Encouragement of *feelings* from the pulpit, at the sickbed, with the dying can be helpful. Modeling of straight-forward, honest communication, leveling with parishioners, allowing tensions to be *talked* through, conflict worked through, airing of news both good and bad before it mushrooms into a "family secret," is a healthy minister's gift to a congregation. A steady, consistent, committed care of parishioners can eventually form a foundation for *trust.*

ACoA in a congregation may have either an underdeveloped sense of responsibility leading to apathy or an overdeveloped sense of responsibility springing from guilt. Ministers may be tempted to take advantage of an ACoA hero-type, not just sharing responsibility but abdicating it, so eagerly does the hero seem to want to serve. The apathetic (from the Greek *a-pathos,* without feeling) whose self-esteem was so damaged growing up may not have the psychic energy to assume their rightful role as church. Authoritarianism in the church may have reinforced these ACoA's learned helplessness. A pastor may invite them to take very small steps toward shared responsibility in the community, but they will need much encouragement.

Authority Issues

Authority is almost always a problem for unrecovering adult children. They may be afraid of, isolated from, and/or acting out against authority. They may react vehemently even to necessary and legitimate authority and/or structure in the community. They may still be traumatized by the inconsistent and often violent use of authority in their alcoholic homes; they were so helpless then as authority punished. Inconsistent structures and rules made them more insecure rather than secure. These ACoA may isolate themselves from pastor and/or pastoral team, no matter how kind and diligent the effort to reach them. If they themselves should snatch authority of some church committee, they may wield it harshly, abdicate it for fear of abusing it, or simply continue a learned role of placating, avoiding conflict at all costs and so slowing or stopping the committee's tasks.

Listening respectfully to their concerns and hopes can remind the adult children that they are indeed adults with wisdom to contribute to the church's decision-making processes. Consensus decisions, subsidiarity, collegiality, and fair, firm and especially consistent limits insisted upon by those in authority can contribute to the healing of the adult child's fear of authority.

Approval Needs

Many of the ACoA's unmet needs of childhood for attention, affection and approval are transferred to the pastor. The inexperienced minister can quickly burn out, frustrated or discouraged because he or she cannot yet distinguish real needs from the gaping neediness of some ACoA which no one can fill, save God alone. "Who can save me from this body of death? (read: neediness) *Only* Christ Jesus!" (Rom 7:24).

It can be threatening for the experienced minister as well to realize that a parishioner is clinging, emotionally dependent. Understanding the phenomenon of transference as a healing opportunity —*if* the minister is clear, open, honest, with self and with the parishioner—can reduce the minister's anxiety. Probably ministers could learn a lot by attending Al-Anon, whether they are ACoA or not, if their boundaries tend to blur, if they take too much "care" of others.

Blurring of Boundaries

It is very important for the minister to sort through, to clarify, and to decide the limits of his or her availability and service, firmly maintaining these boundaries in the face of clever manipulations. Again, this models for the parishioner whose boundaries and identity are amoeba-like that limits are a realistic response to being human, creature, finite.

Pastors do want to foster attachment to the community, but in a healthy system, autonomy and differentiation are equally encouraged. When a variety of gifts and services are offered to the community, then the ordained can do that for which they are ordained: order the gifts of the community, gifts given by the Spirit.

External Referenting[1]

A predominant characteristic of co-dependents is external referenting, looking outside oneself for identity, approval, security. An unsuspecting minister can reinforce that lack of autonomy by making moral and spiritual decisions for people. Laws, dogmas, stages of spiritual development can be clung to by unrecovering ACoA, supposedly to secure their salvation. When ministers empower free and truthful consciences (morality), free and open relationships with God (spirituality), appropriate moral and spiritual responses can be found within a person's own heart. Effective ministry lies in facilitating a person's freedom and free response to God's initiatives in life, in decisions, in prayer.

Loyalty Problems

The family secret can operate in the church community. Even if a pastor is drunk on the altar or a minister is pursuing an extramarital affair, any possibility of scandal whether within a local congregation or worldwide church may be denied, hushed up or even loyally defended by the "troops." Since Pope John XXIII gained all the churches' admiration by declaring that the Roman Catholic Church —and, by extension, the whole body of Christ—is called to continual conversion, some of the defensive loyalty which pitted denominations against one another has abated. We are all *semper reformanda*, always reforming, as church. As the bumper sticker proudly proclaims: Christians are not perfect; we are forgiven.

Part of a false loyalty may lie in fear of conflict. Again, rocking the "ark of Peter" may be too frightening for those whose need to belong obscures the truth of a situation. Better not to question, they think; better even, perhaps, to identify with questionable ideas and values and so be counted loyal. Alert ministers will not be fooled by such fearful loyalty nor threatened by open, honest questioning, a sign of the organization's health.

Communication Problems

Small congregations can act out all kinds of indirect communication. ACoA not in recovery are afraid of truth, may distort it, may even lie, and thus create chaos in a community. A local church will have its blamers and placators, its intellectualizers and distractors. Without trust, board or council or committee meetings may look more like a poker game among enemies than a group searching for consensus. Indirect communication and outright lies to the pastor can rupture community. Manipulation, control based on offering only part of the truth, part of the whole picture, can undercut many worthwhile projects. Pastors who know the untreated ACoA in their congregation can level consistently with such folk and model for them direct, open "speaking the truth in love" (1 Jn).

However, it is not just our parishioners whose co-dependency needs to be examined and worked through. A Roman Catholic priest represents many who call for this examination of church as organization. Father Richard Rohr tells priests and bishops, according to an April 21, 1988 story in the *National Catholic Reporter,* that "the ecclesial system works on co-dependency, with the church and its ministers agreeing to be sick and not to call each other sick, in a tyranny of power, manipulation and control."[2] More recently, Rev. Matthew Fox issued the same challenge to church leaders in his pastoral letter to the Vatican's Cardinal Ratzinger. Fox asks, "Is the Catholic Church a Dysfunctional Family?"[3]

We believe that any worldwide denomination, not just Catholicism, and any local congregation or religious community can carry these seeds of disease within itself. The body of Christ is under the influence of the Holy Spirit. We are prey, however, as a community, to the "flesh," to those parts of ourself as community which are diseased, under the influence of evil, sin and weakness. Thus, to explore church as organization, subject to the conscious evil and unconscious weakness inherent in any organizational system, is in order.

Chapter 17

Church Organization and Addiction

Church as organization can, like an addictive substance, numb its members, encouraging them to escape from the here and now, to await the promises of bliss in the future.[1] This is not the place to discuss religion as a defense against reality. It may be enough to alert ministers not to foster too much identification with the church for those ACoA whose boundaries and identities are amorphous. "Lost souls" may find church a refuge, overachievers may use the organization to gain power over committees and perhaps the pastor as well, placators may search for self-esteem in the "fixing" of flaws.

The Organization Itself as Addicting

For ministers the church as organization may act like an addictive substance as well. *"Anything* can be addictive when it becomes so central in one's life that one feels that life is not possible without the substance or the process."[2] Note: any *thing.* Church is body of Christ, people of God, community of believers, and while some ministers might get hooked by people, acting co-dependently in a blind "service," we focus here on the "thing," the institution, as a possible addictive substance.

For some ministers, the "organization holds lots of promises. It promises that you will get ahead. It promises power, money and influence."[3] In this promise-package, the organization acts like those substances which can make us "high." When I am drinking, alcoholics claim, I feel so powerful, so important. As alcohol and its promised release operates to hold the alcoholic hostage, so church can function, rewarding us for making church the very center of our lives.

This can be particularly seductive to those ministers who do not have much family, nor a happy family. They can make church their primary group and begin to want all their needs met there. Some-times even their inner truth and individual hope gets blotted out as they strain to become the good company man/woman.

The mission of the church is Jesus' own: to preach good news and to heal the broken-hearted. The mission of the organization, as it operates denominationally or even locally, is not always a prolonging of Jesus' mission. What would please the local minister's superiors? Sometimes preaching *good* news can be just as threatening in a dio-cese as it was in Jesus' time. Sometimes church rules can cause more broken hearts than they help. It is a caricature to think of higher authorities always urging a larger collection, the building of a more elaborate church plant, the quieting of dissent, the conformity of the faithful, but each minister could list what specific actions and atti-tudes would bring praise from his or her superiors. According to Schaef and Fassel, the strain eventually tells. "People in the helping professions are often exhausted and depressed. They join an organi-zation to do one thing and spend most of their time doing another . . . frequently . . . totally incongruent with the reasons they became helpers in the first place."[4]

The organization, like society, may promote workaholism. Soci-ety warns us to take care of ourselves—vacation, diet, exercise—and sometimes ministers do try to reduce stress by these means. Some become bulimic in their dieting, some become addicted to exercise. Yet in all this supposed "self-care" lies the trap: we may bolster our health, increase our energy so that we can devote longer hours, more creativity to the organization.

There is a more subtle trap for ministers. We may have preached sermons against that workaholism which promotes the false idol of the big buck, workaholism which keeps parents away from home, not out of love but from fear of marital or family closeness. Because we, however, serve God, not mammon, we may not notice how centered our lives are, not on God, but on church as rewarding/punishing institution. More work gives us a "fix," builds our self-esteem or enhances our martyr role. Whether the business man, the career woman or the church minister, the workaholic needs to numb self from the anxiety, loneliness, low self-opinion, pain which threatens to overwhelm if we stop "dancing as fast as we can."

This is an even deeper snare for the celibate minister. After all, St. Paul encourages celibacy so that all one's energy might be en-tirely devoted to "the Lord's work" (1 Cor 7:32–35). Presumably the married minister's spouse and children exert some here-and-now pressures which keep the demands of ministry from swallowing the minister. The celibate who is unclear in his or her motivations may pride himself or herself on doing the Lord's work, however, twenty hours a day.

The word of God lays bare the motives of the heart (Heb 4:12). As a minister grows in relationship with God, whether through the word who is Jesus or the word of scripture and prayer, motivations do come more clear. Discerning what work is truly the Lord's, what work is a drug against pain, what work fosters co-dependency in those we serve, may require not only a deepening of personal prayer but a reaching out to a spiritual director, ACoA sponsor, or (yes, even *after* seminary) a chosen supervisor. Reflecting with another on work which we may too easily label the Lord's ministry can cut through that ever-lurking defense: denial.

Finally, the workaholic gains his or her identity through immersion in the system/organization/institution. This identity may have been deliberately fostered in seminary or novitiate. Even if it were not, many ministers do come to donate their whole person not to God, not to the people of God, but to the organization. If he or she were suddenly stripped of ordination or expelled from a religious community, if titles of reverend, sister, pastor, father, brother were suddenly banned, what a quaking at the core of the person might arise. Those are drastic cuts to the core. Many ministers are deeply shaken even by a transfer from one local institution to another. "I built this parish." "This is *my* school." "My heart was in this CPE program." To be fired from a local organization such as parish, hospital, school, chaplaincy is even more traumatic when one's whole life has been centered there. The organization/institution has "become an addictive substance."[5]

The Organization as Alcoholic Family

Much of this book can be used in ministry with those adults who grew up in dysfunctional families, families disrupted by death or serious, chronic illness of a parent, by divorce, or similar loss of a parent's physical and/or emotional presence. However, with a progressive, chronic illness such as alcoholism there are certain characteristics of the disease of the parent or parents which impact the family as loss does not. Thus we limit our discussion to the ways in which the church as organization can behave in ways similar to an alcoholic family.

Denial of the disease is key, mushrooming into *the* family secret, skewing trust and communication. The alcoholic and the family become progressively isolated from their own reality—thoughts, feelings, decisions—and from significant interaction outside the family. The alcoholic's self-centeredness drags the family into its vortex, and everyone's mood, energy, self-esteem is fixed on the alcoholic. Alcoholism is a family disease. Whatever disease infects the church as organization, then, affects each member.

In their book,[6] Schaef and Fassel discuss characteristics of an organization which is an addict. Some may apply to the church. Lay minister David Murray also writes in the *National Catholic Reporter* about institutional alcoholism:

> . . . In my opinion, the Catholic church suffers, as an institution, from alcoholism. The behavior and attitudes coming from the hierarchy and embedded within the training of seminarians, the often confusing and inconsistent leadership, the mixed messages, the inability to apologize for its mistakes, its exploitation of the laity, its defensive concern for its own image, its air of superiority—these and much more are closely related to the attitudes and mannerisms of an individual alcoholic.
>
> I would contend that alcohol is a substance in abuse within the church. With such large numbers of clergy using and abusing it, it would seem to me they would inculcate an alcoholic mentality through the policy and leadership they espouse.
>
> I would further suggest that the laity are adult-children of this alcoholic parent. As a whole, we were raised within this alcoholic family system and have adopted the behaviors of an adult child, as well as survival-type behaviors within the church.
>
> I write this because I am an adult-child of an alcoholic parent. I have also been involved in church ministry for over 15 years, graduated from a Catholic high school and am a former seminarian.[7]

Murray, perhaps rightly, attributes much that is harmful to actual substance abuse by church hierarchy and clerics. Even without the abuse of alcohol, organizational hierarchy may behave as alco-

holics. For example, Matthew Fox decided to address Cardinal Ratzinger directly, breaking a pattern inherent in many organizations,
indirect communication. He notes that many criticize the cardinal
behind his back; Fox will dare to speak the truth. "The alcoholic
father, for example, is always appeased and placated in hopes that he
will not become violent yet another time. . . . Servile patience is
a sin."[8]

Written memos, triangulation, avoidance of open conflict and
secrets are all facets of dysfunctional communication, write Schaef
and Fassel. "Decisions about money, salary and personnel are often
secret." They continue: "Families are only as sick as the secrets they
keep. . . . Secrets are divisive and powerful."[9] Secrets engender
feelings of exclusion and helplessness. For example, National Catholic News Service reported in the October 29, 1987 front page story
of Washington, D.C.'s *Catholic Standard:*[10] "Bishops began approv-
ing this week a list of proposals for Pope John Paul II on the role of
the laity in the Church and the world with little chance the proposals
would be published. Voting on the list of secret proposals began
Tuesday, with 'no talk of making it public,' according to the synod's
press officer."

Control

Control is a major factor in an alcoholic home. Everyone tries to
control feelings, drinking, other family members. Rules multiply as a
system sickens.[11] Through impression management, chaos, crisis and
confusion within the family (organization) are minimized, even denied, rather than worked through and healed.

The ultimate in attempts to control and manage impression, both
characteristic of much hierarchical communication, is the need for
perfection. "Perfectionism requires institutionalized secrets and dis-
honesty," write Schaef and Fassel.[12] Hierarchy feels compelled to
cover up mistakes, sometimes to deny even factual realities. All de-
nominational leaders are facing scandals, lawsuits, notoriety in areas
of money (e.g. Jim Bakker, the Vatican Bank), sex (e.g. child moles-
tation, Bakker, Swaggart), power (e.g. malpractice of pastoral counselors).

It is dangerous to proclaim that the church as organization represents God/Christ on earth. The kingdom of God is not co-extensive
with the church. Better to translate "kingdom," a spatial term, as
"reign of God," a process which takes into account God's wonderful

respect for our human freedom. Jesus is the only Lord; God's is the only reign; the head of the body is Christ alone.

All other leadership, all other ruling is relative. Looking in on an alcoholic family, it is clear that alcohol controls the household: the persons, the schedule, the mood, the rules, the rights and responsibilities. The alcoholic is the center of attention. As church communities grow and become more healed of co-dependent behaviors, legitimate authority will be treated more legitimately. Until then, even should highest authorities rant, rave, threaten, or cajole, adult children in recovery will keep the truth of their authority in perspective.

Characteristics of a Healthy Family/System

A healthy family system is characterized by mutual respect between spouses and between parents and children. It is an open society: open expression of thoughts, feelings and conflicts; openly discussed consensual decisions; open to input from outside the system; open to reality. A healthy family provides flexibility, diversity and differentiation. It is detached enough to foster individuality and self-criticism; yet its boundaries are porous enough to nourish intimacy, and to allow interchange of roles and responsibilities. A healthy family does not take itself too seriously.

Church community, even church as organization, cannot be described as family, yet there are similarities. There are healthy congregations and religious communities who have worked through much temptation, tugs of unredeemed elements, conflict, much disease. They would be characterized by mutual respect: member for member, members with ministers, ministers among themselves.

Theirs would be an open society, welcoming new ideas, new members. They would communicate directly, trusting enough not only to share ideas but feelings. They would trust enough to address conflicts head-on and keep on dialoguing until problems were resolved. Consensus government would assure members of their value in making community decisions; decisions would thus be owned by the whole group.

Whatever rules a community of adults might need would be flexible. Diversity of thinking would be encouraged, differentiation of persons welcomed. Old/young, married/single, gay/straight, liberal/conservative, active/contemplative, strong/weak, sick/healthy, introvert/extrovert (etc.) adults would enrich, not threaten, the unity of the community.

Boundaries would be clear. "From each according to his/her ability; to each according to his/her need" is a principle enunciated by Karl Marx yet originating in the Acts of the Apostles (2:45). Each member's gifts for ministry, that is, for the building up of the community, would be nurtured. Subsidiarity, each member working to his or her capacity for the good of the community, without interference in the responsibilities of others, would provide for effective action and adult accountability.

Ministers can facilitate this kind of healthy local church. Thus they prolong and put flesh on Jesus' own mission of setting captives free, teaching and modeling autonomy, differentiation and freedom, the baptismal birthright of the grown-up children of God.

Chapter 18

When Church Leaders Care

As the ACoA movement emerges, many who minister to ministers have come to realize that the roots of much ministerial burn-out dig deep, right back into families of origin. This chapter[1] will be descriptive in hope that bishops, personnel directors, continuing education and formation directors, even those in authority on a local level such as senior pastors or local superiors, may acquire or deepen their (1) understanding that family of origin can still have power over the adult minister; (2) compassion, should a minister ask for treatment; (3) awareness so that we not reinforce behaviors which may be compulsive, pain-filled ways that the minister has for coping; (4) readiness, once an affirming relationship has been established, to raise hard questions for the workaholic or the super-responsible, the unduly ambitious or chaos-creating, the passively silent or passive-aggressive minister.

Authorities who facilitate church ministry, of course, are eager to contribute to the personal health of each minister. In today's church, collegiality and team ministry have sometimes increased stress for the minister, perhaps because one or more team members grew up in a dysfunctional family and are carrying old patterns of relating from family into the workplace.

Effects on the Minister

Society, and often church leaders, can value and reward behaviors which really are symptoms of a continuing disease, as much in need of recovery as alcoholism itself. Even St. Paul boasts about his work in a way which might not be healthy!

> Let me remind you how hard we used to work, slaving night and day so as not to be a burden on any one of you (1 Thess 2:9).

In *Choice Making*,[2] ACoA therapist Sharon Wegscheider-Cruse and her husband Joseph Cruse, a medical doctor, reflect on how society views some of the symptoms and pathology of that disease related to alcoholism, co-dependence and/or para-alcoholism. Some ACoA, para-alcoholics ("para" means resembling alcoholics in behavior), may act-out with violence or substance addictions; some may be sickly or fragile. Some, many who are attracted to ministry, have fulfilled what society calls the American dream. Although driven, harried workaholics, they are considered dedicated and successful. They do not have time for the pain. Although controlling and manipulating others, they are considered strong leaders. The perfectionists are prized as most dependable, the care-takers as loving and reliable, those unable to form close love relationships and/or cooperative work relationships as independent. Those workers (ministers) with undying and often unquestioning loyalty to the organization (church institution) are admired, although in truth they are terrified to risk a criticism, a complaint, even a question lest they be rejected.

Like parents, like society, church leaders may reinforce the successful organizer's workaholism, proudly applaud a macho minister as mature and self-disciplined, intensify the fear of the loyal that they cannot meet the high expectations of the church institutions/authorities. Church leaders may be thoroughly unaware of the loneliness, guilt, feelings of inadequacy, anger and fear such ACoA behaviors can mask.

Masking truth is perhaps the chief problem of the ACoA. Let us examine just a few forms which this distortion of truth can take. The first is extremism in thought and/or behavior. For example, their attitude toward authority, so twisted by an inconsistent use of authority during their most vulnerable years, may lead them to rage, whine, make cynical remarks about or avoid persons with authority. On the other hand, they may fawn over, flatter, ingratiate, wait on or cling to authority figures, seeking continual affirmation. They may shirk responsibility for a project or they may assume, actually usurp, too much responsibility.

Truth was distorted for them as children; as ACoA in the workplace they may unwittingly distort truth through false advertising, promising more than they or their institution can deliver. On the other hand, they may offer less than they can actually deliver because their self-esteem has been so battered. They may exaggerate or self-deprecate. They may collude, sometimes only inchoately knowing that they are involved in a "scheme" their superior has dreamed up. They make excuses not only for themselves but for their superiors (who often continue the role of mother and father to the unaware ACoA), their organizations and/or institutions because of their once-upon-a-time need to protect their parents' good name, their own fragile egos, the institution of the "good Christian family." Sometimes for the ACoA a dysfunctional institution of parish, school, hospital, diocesan office, provincialate, retirement home substitutes for the dysfunctional institution of family. Sometimes, even when there is no need to, ACoA, even ministers, simply lie.

In their distortion of feeling, again ACoA can be extreme in forming work relationships and establishing boundaries between persons, between the self and the institution. ACoA usually do not have a clear sense of individuality, of autonomy. The minister loses himself or herself in the institution, becomes identified with the institution, whether on a local scale or with the institutional church. Getting meaning and identity not just from the work, the service, but service acknowledged by authorities and lauded by the "servees," the minister finds temporary fulfillment, but uses enormous amounts of energy to maintain the gratitude and applause, the preferred way to bolster a weak self-esteem. Because self-esteem is based not on one's own clear and inner self-assessment but on external standards of success, ACoA are thus inordinately crushed by criticism.

On the other hand, some ACoA erect such firm boundaries that they punch clocks, maintain rigid schedules, withhold appropriate feeling from co-workers and those whom they serve. Feelings in an alcoholic home were so chaotic and frightening that such an ACoA defends against emotion by busy-ness. So filled yet with unresolved pain, some ministers quickly band-aid others' pain or even refuse to listen, let alone get involved. Pain at home underlined the child's powerlessness, and such an adult minister, not realizing his or her own new and adult inner resources, may still be raging at our powerless God and at his or her own powerless self.

Boundaries for information are blurred too. Team ministry calls for forthright communication, and yet ACoA were brought up not to talk, to play one's cards close to the vest, to hush up conflict and other family secrets. In reaction to this, some ACoA go to the other extreme, talking without boundaries: engaging in inappropriate self-disclosure, hashing and rehashing, using talk as a defense, nosing into and spreading others' private information. *The Washington Post* (8/26/87, p. A16) quoted an official covering up Oliver North's involvement with the Contras: "My frame of mind was to protect, was to be a member of the team. . . . It's all part of a passivity . . . just to get through troubled waters," he told the House-Senate panels. In that national situation, boundaries of information, authority, responsibility were skewed.

How difficult it is for someone who survived a painful family to enjoy healthy interaction at work. (Even to "enjoy" work for the super-responsible ACoA can be a contradiction in terms!) In an effective ministry, these values are important:

—honesty, and yet truth is so hard for an ACoA to discover;
—creativity, yet an ACoA adhering to institutional customs and codes can be frightened to risk the new;
—clear communication, which means clear feeling, balanced thinking, basic trust, just the opposite of the cardinal rules for ACoA;
—responsible follow-through, which requires reasonable accountability flowing from clear communication;
—appropriate work relationships which means a measure of independent thinking and acting, without considering ministerial colleagues as one's primary group;
—subsidiarity, which may cramp the family hero's ("I'll do it all, leave it to me") style;
—reflection, which short-circuits knee-jerk compulsive reactions;
—collegiality, which sums up all the above.

When ACoA begin to recover, however, authorities and colleagues may find them "difficult." Once ACoA are aware, often after years of repression, of the pain in their family, they cut away the old band-aids and dead skin that covered the wound. That may mean cutting away former styles of being and doing, former friends, bosses, and institutions. With a growing dedication now to truth, they will expect truth from co-workers and authorities. If extremism is tempered, they will not act out their desire for truth with flagrant confrontation, but they will begin to ask the probing question, offer the critique they may previously have swallowed.

Of course extremism may not be tempered in one week or one year. Recovery is a lifelong process. It will probably begin quite messily. Anger may explode, extra responsibility may be rudely refused, personal boundaries may be violated as the non-talker and non-truster swing to the opposite extreme. Truth is in the eventual balance, eventual poise.

What Healing May Look Like

Truth will renew the source of the ACoA's action. Kindness and loyalty gradually will be grounded in reality rather than in fear of losing friends or job. Dependability will stem from interior integrity more than from fear of losing face. Responsibility will be appropriately assumed, although that may mean many "no's" to the extra project, extra hours, extra miles. The person in authority may at first miss being made much of and waited on, but he or she can count on the recovering ACoA's energy to flow into the task at hand.

Energy will flow. Pent-up emotions, especially anger and even fear, have been damming up energy for work. Pent-up trust and talk, once beginning to emerge, will render the minister more honest, simple and free in work relationships. There will be less to protect and thus less defensiveness, hiding out of information, desires and self. Recovering ACoA find themselves more, yet appropriately, available to those they serve, to those they serve with, and, most importantly, to themselves.

Truth sets free. What once crippled can become—gradually— the very source of grace and freedom. When ACoA begin to heal, energy is released, "truth springs up out of the earth." Reflective, dialogic, discerning co-workers for the reign of God are our best hope for renewal of church communities and church structures.

Notes

Chapter 1

[1] Howard J. Clinebell, *Understanding and Counselling the Alcoholic Through Religion and Psychology* (Nashville: Abingdon Press, 1956, 1968).

[2] E.M. Jellinek, *The Disease Concept of Alcoholism* (New Haven: Hillhouse Press, 1960).

[3] Patti McConnell (pseud.), *Adult Children of Alcoholics* (San Francisco: Harper and Row, 1986), p. 120.

[4] Harriet G. Lerner, *The Dance of Anger* (New York: Harper and Row, 1985).

[5] Claudia Black, *It Will Never Happen to Me* (Denver: Medical Administration, 1981).

[6] Virginia Satir, *People-Making* (Palo Alto: Science and Behavior Books, 1972).

[7] Murray Bowen, *Family Therapy in Clinical Practice* (New York: Jason Aronson, 1978).

[8] Lerner, *The Dance of Anger.*

[9] Edwin Friedman, *Generation to Generation: Family Process in Church and Synagogue* (New York: The Guilford Press, 1985), p. 35.

[10] Robert Ackerman, *Children of Alcoholics: A Guidebook for Educators, Therapists and Parents*, 2d ed. (Holmes Beach, Fla.: Learning Publications, 1983).

[11] Janet G. Woititz, *Adult Children of Alcoholics* (Deerfield Beach, Fla.: Health Communications, 1983).

[12] Janet G. Woititz, *Marriage on the Rocks* (New York: Delacorte Press, 1979), p. 129.

Chapter 2

[1] Monica McGoldrick and Randy Gerson, *Genograms in Family Assessment* (New York: W.W. Norton, 1985).

169

Chapter 3

[1] Fran Ferder, *Words Made Flesh* (Notre Dame: Ave Maria Press, 1986).

[2] Anthony de Mello, S.J., *Sadhana: A Way to God* (New York: Doubleday, 1984), pp. 9–55.

[3] David Burns, M.D., *Feeling Good: New Mood Therapy* (New York: Signet, 1980).

[4] Allen Edwards, *Edwards Personal Preference Schedule* (New York: The Psychological Corporation).

[5] William Schutz, *Fundamental Interpersonal Relations Orientation-Behavior* (Consulting Psychologists Press, Inc.).

Chapter 5

[1] David Treadway, "The Tie That Binds," *The Family Therapy Networker*, July/August 1987.

[2] Virginia Satir, quoted by Charles Whitfield at a conference, December 10, 1987, in Washington, D.C.

[3] Lerner, *The Dance of Anger.*

[4] Anne Wilson Schaef and Diane Fassel, *Addictive Organization* (San Francisco: Harper & Row, 1988), p. 189.

[5] Melody Beattie, *Codependent No More: How To Stop Controlling Others and Start Caring for Yourself* (San Francisco: Harper/Hazelden, 1987), pp. 80–81.

[6] De Mello, *Sadhana: A Way to God*, pp. 113–114.

Chapter 7

[1] Rachel Callahan, CSC and Rea McDonnell, SSND, *Hope for Healing: Good News for Adult Children of Alcoholics* (New York: Paulist Press, 1987), pp. 40–41.

[2] Ibid., pp. 50–52.

[3] Ibid., pp. 30–31.

[4] Ibid., p. 40.

[5] Julian of Norwich, *Meditations with Julian of Norwich*, introduction by Brendan Doyle (Santa Fe: Bear and Company, 1983), p. 99. "Jesus is our true Mother in whom we are endlessly carried and out of whom we will never come."

[6] Harold Kushner, *When Bad Things Happen to Good People* (New York: Avon, 1983).

[7] Douglas John Hall, *God and Human Suffering* (Minneapolis: Augsburg, 1986).

[8] John Herder, *Tao of Leadership: Leadership Strategies for a New Age* (New York: Bantam Books, 1985).

[9] Brian McDermott, S.J., *What Are They Saying About the Grace of Christ?* (New York: Paulist Press, 1984).

[10] Anne Wilson Schaef, *Co-Dependence: Misunderstood, Mistreated* (Minneapolis: Winston, 1986), p. 46.

Chapter 8

[1] Ernesto Cardenal, *The Gospel in Solentiname*, 4 vols. (Maryknoll, N.Y.: Orbis Press, 1976).

[2] Thomas Groome, *Christian Religious Education* (San Francisco: Harper and Row, 1980).

[3] Louis Monden, *Sin, Liberty, and Law* (New York: Sheed and Ward, 1965).

Chapter 9

[1] Laurence Brammer, *The Helping Relationship: Process and Skills*, (Englewood Cliffs: Prentice-Hall, 1972); R. Carkhuff and B. Berensen, *Beyond Counseling and Psychotherapy* (New York: Holt, Rinehart and Winston, 1967); Gerard Egan, *The Skilled Helper* (Belmont: Wadsworth, 1982); Fran Ferder, *Words Made Flesh* (Notre Dame: Ave Maria Press, 1986); Eugene Kennedy, *On Becoming A Counselor* (New York: Seabury, 1977).

[2] A. Ivey, *Microcounseling: Interviewing Skills Manual* (Springfield: C.C. Thomas, 1972).

Chapter 10

[1] Gerald Caplan, *Principles of Preventive Psychiatry* (New York: Basic Books, 1964).

[2] Erich Lindemann, "Symptomatology and Management of Acute Grief," in *Crisis Intervention: Selected Readings*, H. Parad, ed. (New York: Family Services Association of America, 1965), pp. 7–21.

[3] Caplan, *Principles*.

[4] Reuben Hill, "Generic Features of Families Under Stress," in Parad, *op. cit.*, pp. 32–52.

[5] Naomi Golan, *Treatment in Crisis Situations* (New York: Free Press, 1978).

[6] *Ibid.*

[7] Emily Marlin, *Hope: New Choices and Recovery Strategies for Adult Children of Alcoholics* (San Francisco: Harper & Row, 1987), p. 22.

[8] Christine Courtois, *Healing the Incest Wound*, (New York: Norton, 1988), pp. 137–139.

Chapter 11

[1] For example, Howard J. Clinebell, *Basic Types of Pastoral Counseling* (Nashville: Abingdon, 1984) and Barry K. Estadt, editor, *Pastoral Counseling* (Englewood Cliffs: Prentice-Hall, 1983).

[2] Emily Marlin, *Hope: New Choices and Recovery Strategies for Adult Children of Alcoholics* (New York: Harper and Row, 1987), pp. 254–265; Charles Whitfield, *Healing the Child Within* (Pompano Beach: Health Communications, 1987), pp. 2–4.

[3] Black, *It Will Never Happen to Me.*

[4] Whitfield, *Healing the Child Within*, p. 40.

[5] American Psychiatric Association, *DSM III, Diagnostic and Statistical Manual of Mental Disorders*, 3rd ed. (Washington, D.C.: American Psychiatric Press, 1980), pp. 236–238.

[6] Whitfield, *Healing the Child Within*, pp. 43–44.

[7] Janet Woititz, *Struggle for Intimacy* (Pompano Beach: Health Communications, 1985).

[8] Lerner, *The Dance of Anger.*

[9] Burns, *Feeling Good: New Mood Therapy.*

Chapter 12

[1] *Alcoholics Anonymous: The Story of How Many Thousands of Men and Women Have Recovered from Alcoholism*, 3d ed. (New York: Alcoholics Anonymous World Services, Inc., 1976), pp. 1–16.

[2] Monden, *Sin, Liberty, and Law.*

[3] Patrick McCloskey, O.F.M., *When You Are Angry with God* (New York: Paulist Press, 1987).

[4] Pierre Wolff, S.J., *May I Hate God?* (New York: Paulist Press, 1979).

[5] Rea McDonnell, SSND, *The Catholic Epistles and Hebrews* (Wilmington: Michael Glazier, Inc., 1986), pp. 96–97.

[6] De Mello, *Sadhana: A Way to God.*

[7] Laurence Dunlop, *Patterns of Prayer in the Psalms* (New York: Seabury, 1982).

[8] Rea McDonnell, SSND, *Prayer Pilgrimage Through Scripture* (New York: Paulist Press, 1984), pp. 63–64.

[9] Ibid., p. 63.
[10] Ibid., pp. 89–90.
[11] Ibid., pp. 64–65.

Chapter 13

[1] Ferder, *Words Made Flesh.*
[2] *Alcoholics Anonymous: The Story of How Many Thousands Have Recovered from Alcoholism,* p. 13.
[3] Thomas H. Green, S.J., *Weeds Among the Wheat* (Notre Dame: Ave Maria Press, 1984), pp. 61–62.

Chapter 16

[1] Schaef, *Co-Dependence,* p. 44.
[2] Richard Rohr, O.F.M., in *National Catholic Reporter,* April 21, 1988.
[3] Matthew Fox, O.P., in *Creation,* November/December 1988, p. 28.

Chapter 17

[1] Anne Wilson Schaef and Diane Fassel, *The Addictive Organization: Why We Overwork, Cover Up, Pick Up the Pieces, Please the Boss and Perpetuate Sick Organizations* (San Francisco: Harper and Row, 1988), pp. 118–136.
[2] Ibid., p. 119.
[3] Ibid.
[4] Ibid., p. 123.
[5] Ibid., p. 136.
[6] Ibid., pp. 137–176.
[7] David Murray in *National Catholic Reporter,* April 21, 1988.
[8] Fox, *Creation,* p. 29.
[9] Schaef and Fassel, *The Addictive Organization,* pp. 139–141.
[10] "The Catholic Standard," Vol. 37, No. 44 (October 29, 1987), p. 1.
[11] Schaef and Fassel, *The Addictive Organization,* p. 164.
[12] Ibid., p. 152.

Chapter 18

[1] Much of this chapter has been reprinted with permission of the National Association of Church Personnel Administrators. It ap-

peared in the October 1987 issue of *Church Personnel Issues* as "Working Toward Freedom: Hope for Adult Children of Alcoholics," by Rea McDonnell, SSND.

[2] Sharon Wegscheider-Cruse, *Choice-Making* (Pompano Beach: Health Communications, 1985).

Bibliography

Ackerman, Robert. *Children of Alcoholics: A Guidebook for Educators, Therapists and Parents.* 2d ed. Holmes Beach: Learning Publications, 1983.

Alcoholics Anonymous: The Story of How Many Thousands of Men and Women Have Recovered from Alcoholism. 3d ed. New York: Alcoholics Anonymous World Services, Inc., 1976.

Beattie, Melody. *Co-Dependent No More: How To Stop Controlling Others and Start Caring for Yourself.* San Francisco: Harper/Hazelden, 1987.

Becker, Ernest. *The Denial of Death.* New York: The Free Press, 1973.

Bowen, Murray. *Family Therapy in Clinical Practice.* New York: Jason Aronson, 1978.

Brammer, Lawrence. *The Helping Relationship: Process and Skills.* Englewood Cliffs: Prentice-Hall, 1973.

Burns, David. *Feeling Good: New Mood Therapy.* New York: Signet, 1980.

Black, Claudia. *It Will Never Happen to Me.* Colorado: Medical Administration, 1981.

Callahan, Rachel, CSC, and McDonnell, Rea, SSND. *Hope for Healing: Good News for Adult Children of Alcoholics.* New York: Paulist Press, 1987.

Caplan, Gerald. *Principles of Preventive Psychiatry.* New York: Basic Books, 1964.

Capps, Donald. *Pastoral Counseling and Preaching: A Quest for an Integrated Ministry.* Philadelphia: Westminster, 1980.

Cardenal, Ernesto. *The Gospel in Solentiname.* 4 vols. Maryknoll: Orbis Press, 1976.

Carkhuff, R.; and Berenson, B. *Beyond Counseling and Psychotherapy.* New York: Holt, Rinehart and Winston, 1967.

Clinebell, Howard J. *Understanding and Counseling the Alcoholic.* Nashville: Abingdon, 1956, 1968.

————. *Basic Types of Pastoral Counseling.* Nashville: Abingdon, 1984.

Coleman, Sally. *Lifework: Adult Children of Alcoholics Group Manual.* Notre Dame: Ave Maria Press, 1988.

Courtois, Christine. *Healing the Incest Wound.* New York: Norton, 1988.

Dean, Amy E. *Once Upon A Time: Stories From Adult Children.* Minnesota: Hazelden, 1987.

De Mello, Anthony, S.J. *Sadhana: A Way to God.* New York: Doubleday, 1984.

Deutsch, C. *Broken Bottles, Broken Dreams: Understanding and Helping the Children of Alcoholics.* New York: Teachers College Press, 1982.

The Dilemma of the Alcoholic Marriage. An anonymous author from Al-Anon. New York: Alanon Family Group Headquarters, Inc. 13th printing, 1987.

Dunlop, Laurence. *Patterns of Prayer in the Psalms.* New York: Seabury, 1982.

Egan, Gerard. *The Skilled Helper.* Belmont: Wadsworth, 1982.

Estadt, B.K., ed. *Pastoral Counseling.* Englewood Cliffs: Prentice-Hall, Inc., 1983.

Ferder, Fran. *Words Made Flesh.* Notre Dame: Ave Maria Press, 1986.

Friedman, Edwin. *Generation to Generation: Family Process in Church and Synagogue.* New York: Guilford Press, 1985.

Golan, Naomi. *Treatment in Crisis Situations.* New York: Free Press, 1978.

Gravitz, Herbert and Bowden, Julie. *Guide to Recovery: A Book for Adult Children of Alcoholics.* Holmes Beach: Learning Publications, 1985.

Green, Thomas H., S.J. *Weeds Among the Wheat.* Notre Dame: Ave Maria Press, 1984.

Groome, Thomas. *Christian Religious Education.* San Francisco: Harper and Row, 1980.

Hall, Douglas John. *God and Human Suffering.* Minneapolis: Augsburg, 1986.

Heider, John. *Tao of Leadership: Leadership Strategies for a New Age.* New York: Bantam Books, 1985.

Helfer, Ray, M.D. *Childhood Comes First.* 2d ed. East Lansing: Ray Helfer, 1978, 1984.

Hill, Reuben. "Generic Features of Families Under Stress." In H.

Parad (ed.), *Crisis Intervention: Selected Readings.* New York: Family Services Association of America, 1967, pp. 32–57.

Ivey, A. *Microcounseling: Interviewing Skills Manual.* Springfield: C.C. Thomas, 1972.

Jellinek, E.M. *The Disease Concept of Alcoholism.* New Haven: Hillhouse Press, 1960.

Kennedy, Eugene. *On Becoming A Counselor.* New York: Seabury, 1977.

Kritsberg, Wayne. *Adult Children of Alcoholics Syndrome.* Pompano Beach: Health Communications Inc., 1985.

Kushner, Harold S. *When Bad Things Happen to Good People.* New York: Avon, 1983.

Lerner, Harriet Goldhor. *The Dance of Anger.* New York: Harper and Row, 1985.

Lindemann, Erich. "Symptomatology and Management of Acute Grief." In H. Parad (ed.), *Crisis Intervention: Selected Readings.* New York: Family Services Association of America, 1967, pp. 7–21.

Linn, Dennis, S.J. and Linn, Matthew, S.J. *Healing Life's Hurts: Healing Memories Through the Five Stages of Forgiveness.* New York: Paulist Press, 1978.

Marlin, Emily. *Hope: New Choices and Recovery Strategies for Adult Children of Alcoholics.* San Francisco: Harper and Row, 1987.

McCloskey, Patrick, O.F.M. *When You Are Angry With God.* New York: Paulist Press, 1987.

McConnell, Patty (pseud). *A Workbook for Healing: Adult Children of Alcoholics.* San Francisco: Harper and Row, 1986.

McDermott, Brian, S.J. *What Are They Saying About the Grace of Christ?* New York: Paulist Press, 1984.

McDonnell, Rea, SSND. *Prayer Pilgrimage Through Scripture.* New York: Paulist Press, 1984.

———. *The Catholic Epistles and Hebrews.* Wilmington: Michael Glazier, Inc., 1986.

McGoldrick, Monica; and Gerson, Randy. *Genograms in Family Assessment.* New York: W.W. Norton, 1985.

Monden, Louis. *Sin, Liberty, and Law.* New York: Sheed and Ward, 1965.

Napier, Augustus Y., and Whitaker, Carl, M.D. *The Family Crucible.* New York: Bantam Books, 1980.

Satir, Virginia. *Peoplemaking.* Palo Alto: Science & Behavior Books, Inc., 1972.

————. *Conjoint Family Therapy.* Palo Alto: Science & Behavior Books, Inc., 1967.

Schaef, Anne Wilson. *Co-Dependence: Misunderstood, Mistreated.* Minneapolis: Winston, 1986.

————. *When Society Becomes an Addict.* San Francisco: Harper and Row, 1987.

————, and Fassel, Diane. *The Addictive Organization: Why We Overwork, Cover Up, Pick Up The Pieces, Please the Boss and Perpetuate Sick Organizations.* San Francisco: Harper and Row, 1988.

Schutz, William. *Fundamental Interpersonal Relations Orientation-Behavior.* Consulting Psychologists Press, Inc.

Springer, Barbara, S.S.J. "Co-Dependent Adult Children of Alcoholics." Washington, D.C.: Religious Formation Conference, 1986.

Treadway, David. "The Ties that Bind." *The Family Therapy Networker.* July/August 1987.

Viorst, Judith. *Necessary Losses: The Loves, Illusions, Dependencies and Impossible Expectations That All of Us Have to Give Up in Order to Grow.* New York: Simon and Schuster, 1986.

Wegscheider-Cruse, Sharon. *Choice-Making: For Co-Dependents, Adult Children and Spirituality Seekers.* Pompano Beach: Health Communications, 1985.

Whitfield, Charles. *Alcoholism, Other Drug Problems, and Other Attachments and Spirituality: Stress Management and Serenity During Recovery, A Transpersonal Approach.* Baltimore: The Resource Group, 1985.

————. *Healing the Child Within.* Pompano Beach: Health Communications, 1987.

Woititz, Janet. *Marriage on the Rocks.* New York: Delacorte Press, 1979.

————. *Struggle for Intimacy.* Pompano Beach: Health Communications, 1985.

————. *Adult Children of Alcoholics.* Pompano Beach: Health Communications, 1983.

Wolff, Pierre, S.J. *May I Hate God?* New York: Paulist Press, 1979.

Further References

American Psychiatric Association DSM-III. *Diagnostic and Statistical Manual of Mental Disorders.* 3d ed. Washington, D.C.: American Psychiatric Press, 1980.

Lovinger, Robert J. *Working with Religious Issues in Therapy.* New York: Jason Aronson, Inc., 1984.
Robinson, Lillian, ed. *Psychiatry and Religion: Overlapping Concerns.* Washington: American Psychiatric Press, Inc., 1986.

Resources

Adult Children of Alcoholics (ACA—Central Service Board), Box 35623, Los Angeles, California.
Al-Anon Family Groups, P.O. Box 182, Madison Square Station, New York, N.Y. 10159.
National Association for Children of Alcoholics, 31706 Coast Highway, Suite 201, South Laguna, California 92677. (714-499-3889).
National Council on Alcoholism, 12 Twenty-First Street, New York, N.Y. 10010. (212-206-6770).

7241   7690